Praise for Gabrielle Hartley

The Secret to Getting Along

"A very thoughtful, practical, and upbeat book! There are many tips and tools you can learn to apply to any relationship or friendship. By starting with self-awareness, the author brings greater clarity to our own part in relationships conflicts. We are often part of the problem and changing our own approach is so much easier than trying to change the other person (which never works). If you like steps and lists for self-improvement, you will find that Hartley's 3-step method is easy and rewarding to apply."

—Bill Eddy, author of *It's All Your Fault: 12 Tips for Managing People Who Blame Others for Everything* and Chief Innovation Officer of High Conflict Institute

"*The Secret to Getting Along (And Why it's Easier Than You Think)* is a wise and engaging book that should be required reading for anyone in any kind of relationship. All relationships have conflict, but fights and disputes don't have to tear friends apart. Hartley shares practical tips for how to manage and resolve conflicts in a healthy way so that bonds are strengthened rather than frayed."

—Emily Esfahani Smith, author of *The Power of Meaning*

"There are several gems in this book, but what stands out the most is Gabrielle's focus on the need for self-awareness—becoming more capable of recognizing the impact of our actions on others. It is clear that *not* being aware is a major source of conflict and by holding a mirror up to ourselves, we not only improve our capacity to manage conflict, but puts us on a path to our own growth and development.

—Donna Hicks, PhD, author of *Dignity: Its Essential Role in Resolving Conflict*

"Gabrielle Hartley's new book is a smart, instructive, and engaging guide for anyone who is ready to start addressing conflict in their relationships with a holistic approach. It's easy and habitual for people to point fingers and place blame without pausing to consider a more nuanced 360-degree approach that takes the other side's point of view into consideration. Gabrielle's conversational style of writing make reading this book feel more like chatting with a good friend; she lit up my brain with ideas about how I can be working to reduce strife to make my relationships more harmonious and meaningful. Whether you're trying to improve your marriage or address issues more peaceably with an ex or friends or family, this book has invaluable advice."

—Laura Friedman Williams, author of *Available: A Very Honest Account of Life After Divorce*

"*The Secret to Getting Along* is a smart, comprehensive, user-friendly guide for navigating conflict to enjoy healthy relationships with not only other people, but also ourselves. Hartley gives us specific, time-tested tools and insights, culled from her deep experience as a professional mediator, that allow us to make good choices in service of both our own sanity and in keeping the people who matter in our lives, even when we disagree. I can't recommend this book enough, especially in these conflict-riddled times, when our impulses are to either argue with or walk away from those who don't share our beliefs. Chock full of stories, exercises, and useful details, it's a great read!"

—Jill Sherer Murray, award-winning journalist and author
of *Big Wild Love: The Unstoppable Power of Letting Go*

"I wish everyone would read this book before they come into my office. I often see people giving up on relationships because of a conflict they just couldn't resolve. *The Secret to Getting Along (And Why it's Easier Than You Think)* offers step-by-step tools to manage conflict and move through it so you can actually have greater connection. The goal is not to win but to feel seen and heard. Gabrielle has done it again with another pivotal book."

—Elizabeth Cohen, PhD, clinical psychologist and
author of *Light at the Other Side of Divorce*

"It really is easier than you think to avoid conflict and get along better. In this book, Gabrielle Hartley shows you how."
—Lisa Zeiderman,Esq. Managing Partner of Miller Zeiderman LLP

"Conflict is bound to happen but Gabrielle's method provides real, actionable tips for how to avoid it and to keep your team working together and truly getting along"

—David Duncan, President and CEO, First Hospitality

"Reading this book will change everything you thought you knew about conflict resolution and how to actually get along better."

—Natasha Sizlo, author *All Signs Point To:*
A Memoir of Love, Loss and Paris

"Gabrielle Hartley's approach to conflict resolution is simple, effective, and potentially life-changing. A must-read in this world that feels increasingly at odds!"

—Susan Guthrie, Esq., co-founder and
CEO, Mosten Guthrie Academy

Better Apart

"Potent, accessible tools for your family and your future."

—Gwyneth Paltrow

"Think of it as the 'conscious uncoupling' how-to."

—*People*

"In their new book, *Better Apart*, Gabrielle Hartley and Elena Brower advise those going through a separation to employ the wisdom of Marie Kondo... [saying] Kondo's technique can help anyone in the midst of a breakup, whether it's a messy divorce or a heartbreaking split."

—*New York Post*

"Addressing the practical, emotional, and spiritual, *Better Apart* is a major paradigm shifter. As a child of divorce, the lessons within this book resonated deeply with me, and I'm hopeful for the future of separating families who'll have access to this wisdom."

—Kate Northrup, bestselling author of *Money: A Love Story*

"By encouraging parents to forget perfection and establish clear rules and workable schedules, this book demonstrates that some families can truly be better apart."

—Dr. Sharon Saline, clinical psychologist and author
of *What Your ADHD Child Wishes You Knew*

"Gabrielle and Elena provide a warm and thoughtful approach to divorce that includes both legal wisdom and healthy psychological principles. Their discussion of custody and co-parenting leads you on the path toward a calmer and happier future for you and your children."

—Robyn Landow, PhD, psychologist and parenting coordinator

"Gabrielle inspires and educates with a practical, accessible approach, empowering readers to think beyond blame, shame, and anger, and instead focus on personal growth, financial integrity, and a peaceful reorganization of the family unit. This book is a must read for those looking for a roadmap to a better, happier, healthier life post-divorce."

—Marcelle Kott, Esq., Partner, Berger Schatz, Chicago, Illinois

"*Better Apart* is my top recommendation for anyone who is wrestling with the 'divorce' question but feeling shame or fear around it. Gabrielle sets out a doable approach to not just survive divorce, but to thrive emotionally, financially, and spiritually in life after separation. Her thoughtful but practical book lays out a roadmap for using crisis as a unique opportunity for mindful living and personal growth. An amicable divorce truly is possible, and Gabrielle lays out the steps to get there without sacrificing your well-being."

—Erin Levin, Esq. CFLS, CEO of Hello Divorce
and Levine Family Law Group

Also by Gabrielle Hartley

Better Apart: The Radically Positive Way to Separate

The Secret to
GETTING
ALONG

(And Why It's EASIER Than You Think)

3 STEPS TO LIFE-CHANGING CONFLICT RESOLUTION

GABRIELLE HARTLEY

Published by Sourcebooks
P.O. Box 4410, Naperville, Illinois 60567-4410
(630) 961-3900
sourcebooks.com

Originally published in 2023 in the United States of America by Sourcebooks.

Cataloging-in-Publication Data is on file with the Library of Congress.

Printed and bound in the United States of America.
SB 10 9 8 7 6 5 4 3 2 1

This book is dedicated to you, the reader, with the hope that it helps you to get along better with the people in your life that matter.

Contents

Introduction

Hillary and Simone had been best friends since high school. After graduation, they attended the same cosmetology school. While renting chairs side by side at a local salon, they developed a business plan and went on to purchase a hair salon in Chicago. One decade later, their salon boasted a top-notch team of stylists, and they were typically booked out weeks in advance. Their staff was happy, the money was flowing in, and they had a loyal client base. By all markers, these best friends had created a stellar business together.

Hillary couldn't have been happier. She was doing what she'd always dreamed of doing: earning a comfortable salary and working with her best friend. Simone was also satisfied with the salon...at least she had been for the first few years. While she had loved developing the business into a thriving enterprise, she began to feel a growing dissatisfaction every time she walked into the salon. She wanted more. What was once fun suddenly felt humdrum. She began to nurture aspirations of earning more money and operating the salon on a much larger scale.

Over drinks, Simone raised the subject of business expansion with Hillary, starting with moving the business to a better location. Hillary immediately replied that it would be "awesome" to move the business. Simone came away feeling like she and Hillary were both excited about the idea. Yet, unbeknownst to Simone, Hillary was expressing excitement without attaching any actual intention to move the business. Though proud of the business and every bit as passionate about it as Simone, she didn't feel the same urge to expand. When Simone suggested the idea, Hillary didn't want to shoot it down and disappoint her friend. She thought Simone might forget about it, and the two could continue with their successful business venture.

For Simone, however, "awesome" was all she needed. She took the ball and ran with it, immediately setting out to find the perfect new location. Within a month, she found the ideal spot, but to her surprise and dismay, Hillary avoided signing the lease until the space was no longer available. Two months later, the same thing happened with a different space—this time, Simone didn't just lose another lease, she also was about to lose a business contact who had been helping her scout for new locations. Simone angrily blamed Hillary for being slow to sign the lease yet again, then she reacted with outrage when Hillary expressed confusion about the problem.

Hillary didn't understand why Simone was so frustrated. To her, Simone had impulsively charged forward before they'd had any serious conversation about making such a big change. But from Simone's point of view, they'd made a joint decision to move forward. Simone felt so aggravated that she could hardly bring herself to talk to Hillary.

From there, Hillary and Simone's partnership and decades-long friendship quickly unraveled. Hillary bought out Simone's interest in the business, and Simone left to strike out on her own. Even though she had retained the staff and client list, Hillary lacked Simone's business smarts and financially mismanaged the salon until she had no option but to close it. Simone had an equally rough time of it because without Hillary's perceptiveness, she was ill-equipped to hire talented stylists who would attract more clientele.

But perhaps more importantly, Hillary and Simone lost what might have otherwise been a cherished lifelong friendship with each other. What could have been a thoughtful conversation about the future direction of a successful business built by two smart, accomplished women who truly cared about each other became an argument that ended up derailing their personal and professional relationship. The women failed to meaningfully communicate with each other. They made assumptions, became defensive, blamed each other, and eventually cut each other off.

What happened to Hilary and Simone has always been

a natural part of our basic human communication failure—
and now, it has become far too common. What starts as disagreement morphs into senseless argument loops that upend
business partnerships, friendships, and marriages. And, in
our increasingly isolated bubbles, we're less likely to make the
effort to repair these rifts than ever before. Few among us need
to be reminded that we're experiencing unprecedented levels
of interpersonal tension, disagreement, and disinclination to
meaningfully engage with each other amid conflict. Long-
standing family gatherings have been canceled over COVID-
19 vaccination or mask debates. Political disagreements have
dismantled decades-long friendships. We fight over politics,
money, personal health decisions, parenting, and so much
more, leaving everyone lonelier and more susceptible to mental
health issues such as depression and anxiety than ever before.[i]

But in focusing on our increased polarization, or chalking
everything up to "these crazy times," we're overlooking an even
more worrisome part of the equation: **We have gotten really,
really bad at managing conflict. Somewhere along the way,
we've forgotten that some level of disagreement is normal
and even necessary in our relationships.** We've normalized
a zero-sum approach to interpersonal conflict and prioritized
"winning" at all costs. While being right may be satisfying, it's
not going to do much for us in the long run, especially when
it comes to compassion, connection, and community. Even
so, we've become deeply attached to our positions, leaving us

worse listeners than ever before. Moreover, we feel helpless in the face of all the conflict infiltrating every facet of our lives at home, work, and online.

Fortunately, we have tremendous agency to remake our relationship with conflict—and to emerge as stronger, calmer, and kinder people. This book will give you the transformative mind-set and skills needed to embrace and then move beyond personal and professional conflict—using the same methods I've conceptualized and successfully utilized in my law and mediation practice for over two decades.

Welcome to the YES Method

When I was thirty years old, I clerked for a divorce court judge in New York City. I could never have imagined how much I would love—and excel at—bringing a messy divorce to a relatively tidy close. Weaving together a resolution that was accepted by both aggressive attorneys and angry clients became my calling.

When I married my husband and relocated from Brooklyn to Northampton, Massachusetts, I opened a private mediation practice centered on alternative dispute resolution, which meant I was able to work collaboratively with the attorneys on the other side to reach reasonable resolutions. Together, we were able to support our clients in reaching a compromise that each party could live with rather than trying to "win" the most points in court. Today, I have expanded my mediation practice online to help people around the country reach the best possible outcome for their conflict-filled divorce. Sometimes there are lawyers involved; often, it's just two people trying to close a difficult chapter of their lives without destroying each other in the process. In either case, I work with them carefully to arrive at a solution using a structure called the *YES Method* that can be applied to your everyday conflict, which we'll explore in the coming chapters. Spoiler alert: navigating conflict better all begins with *you*. The secret to getting along is something everyone can access, even in the most entrenched arguments. The best part of this method is that it is super doable because it prescribes small changes that result in big outcomes. Of course, you will have to really engage in the three steps and be mindful of them each time you find yourself in a conflict. Once you begin engaging with the YES Method, you will see that getting along better, if not perfectly, is attainable in most relationships. More on this in a moment...

In 2019, I published my first book, *Better Apart: The Radically Positive Way to Separate,* to help readers avoid contentious and destructive conflict in divorce. I focused *Better Apart* around five essential elements: patience, respect, peace, clarity, and forgiveness. By using these five lenses, I helped people going through divorce reconsider how they were handling their process at every step along the way. I've since given dozens of talks and interviews focused on changing the divorce conversation by helping couples get through divorce with ease, grace, and personal power.

After the publication of *Better Apart*, though, something strange happened: past and present clients, along with many of my friends and colleagues, weren't just approaching me to ask for guidance on their divorce cases—they also wanted help managing the conflict disrupting other relationships in their lives. I felt this called for a different tool kit than the one I prescribed in *Better Apart*, which was structured to help readers move forward after a relationship had already irreversibly broken down. I wanted to create a program for developing a healthier relationship with conflict altogether, one that was easy to grasp but would spur deep thought and foundational change.

It was at this time that I began to codify the three steps that I had been intuitively using in mediation for more than two decades. I realized that I often employed these steps to stop conflict from destroying relationships. By walking people through these same steps, I thought, I might be able to help them navigate a wide array of situations in their lives that were stirring up conflict, from coping with household tiffs to dealing with their beloved-yet-hot-headed friends and relatives who held what they deemed obnoxious political perspectives. I came to call this the YES Method.

Y stands for *your* role in the conflict.

E is for the *emotional* story.

S stands for *shelving* heated conversations.

By integrating these three accessible skills, the YES Method has the power to stop all manner of conflict in its tracks and keep it from escalating into all-out chaos. It prevents us from being overly reactive to conflict and cutting ties with people who have been an important part of our lives. It can provide us with other, better options besides ignoring, avoiding, or escalating the point of contention—options that can open pathways to greater togetherness. And, perhaps most importantly, it encourages the type of self-reflection and challenging emotional work that encourages serious personal growth. In these pages, I will counsel you that before you consider canceling a friend, writing off a relative, quitting a job, or leaving a marriage, you should first try saying YES to looking at conflict differently.

To be clear, I'm not talking about slapping a smile on an ugly situation, nor burying your head in the sand around secrets and lies. I'm also not suggesting that this Method is an alternative to counseling or therapy. There are many serious, traumatic, and difficult life situations and experiences that will require professional help beyond what is offered on these pages. I also acknowledge that my privileged life has given me a particular viewpoint and limitation in experience. That said, so long as your basic needs are met and you are not engaged in an abusive relationship, you will see that by engaging in these three simple steps, you have the ability to truly feel better and live with far less circular and unnecessary conflict in every facet of your life.

With the YES Method, I will show you how to build cooperative, thriving relationships amid tensions at work, across conflicting political opinions, and over the endless debates on how to parent—or how to load the dishwasher. Whether you're at the divorce mediation table, the kitchen table, or the virtual table in the comments section, getting along *better* is possible, and it's easier than you think. Through exercises, stories, conversation openers, and other practical tools, you will learn to stay calm and balanced even when facing the most uncomfortable conversations or explosive interpersonal situations. Again, I would like to emphasize that if you are in an abusive relationship, walking away is the only answer. But often, in many scenarios, we have the power to shift our dynamic in surprising ways that are feasible, and supportive of our well-being as well as the health of our relationships over the longer term.

The YES Method isn't going to give you immediate, everlasting peace in all relationships, much less resolve all your conflict. However, it will give you the tools you need to get closer to having higher function within complicated interpersonal dynamics. The fact is, peace and resolution are often fleeting, especially when we're facing entrenched conflict with those in our innermost circles. My goal is to help you achieve emotional freedom—what I call "equanimity"—from conflict. This freedom allows us to look at the big picture, approach conflict with a greater sense of neutrality, and achieve more satisfying compromises and conclusions. Instead of spending hours replaying arguments over and over in your head, mourning friendships that crumbled after unforgivable blow-ups, or circling around the same points of contention for weeks, months, or even years, you'll instead learn to accept conflict as part of every relationship—and use it as a valuable opportunity to grow and achieve balance in your life.

Finding equanimity starts with looking inward. Though many of us think of conflict as outward-facing, the truth is that our experience of conflict is largely subjective and springs from our internal perceptions, habits, and narratives. In other words, conflict happens not only because of a difference of opinion on a matter; it can also arise due to the deep-seated habits, perceptions, and mind-sets that govern everything we do.[ii]

The YES Method is neither a purely prescriptive guide to mediation nor about getting what you "want" out of conflict. Rather, it is a method that is designed to help you make your relationships better and, maybe more importantly, to reach a state of inner balance. Noticing where we hit a wall of disagreement with others (and within ourselves) is illuminating. It is an opportunity both to reach greater understanding of what makes us tick as well as to successfully navigate the sometimes incredibly annoying world around us.

As you go through these pages, you will start to become more aware of your role in your conflict, and you'll receive coaching to help you examine how your habitual ways of thinking, acting, and reacting are contributing to your conflict.

This inner clarity offers a pathway for recalibrating your relationships from the inside out. You will learn to unpack the emotional story and shelve heated conversations to avoid unnecessary or unproductive conversations. As you read on and embrace the YES Method, you will **see how small changes have big impact**. And you will become more self-aware, more thoughtful, and more finely attuned to the bigger picture as you navigate the pitfalls and obstacles of life and human relationships.

The Secret: The YES Method

The YES Method consists of three key steps: understanding *your* role in the conflict (your part of the dynamic, your relationship goals, and your attitudes and habits), unpacking the *emotional* story (understanding each other's true needs and our own inner narratives), and *shelving* (implementing pausing behaviors tailored to reroute potential conflict and to make conversations go more smoothly). These steps have an intentional progression from inner agency to outer behavior.

Recognizing that conflict is a gift that helps a relationship evolve has enabled me to resolve hundreds of complex mediations. Better yet, it has allowed me to maintain a rich network of friends and colleagues who have vastly different viewpoints from me and one another. The YES Method encourages more measured interactions, deeper conversations, and, most of all, an emotionally uplifting sense of equanimity at home, at work, and in life. By using the YES Method, you will gain a renewed ability to engage with your inner self and the world around you.

Even when the most seismic discord breaks loose—pandemics, political divisions, and institutional wrongdoings—you can always turn to the YES Method. The most exciting part of the YES Method is that the process fundamentally changes how we interact with and respond to others without us having to change a thing in our lives—other than our minds. It's a roadmap to free you from the quagmire of seemingly unmanageable conflict.

To help you learn and implement the YES Method in your life, *The Secret to Getting Along (And Why It's Easier Than You Think)* is divided into four sections: "Part I: Your Role in the Conflict," "Part II: The Emotional Story," "Part III: Shelving Heated Conversations," and the secret weapon at the end of the book: "Part IV: Yes, You Can Get Along."

Part I: Your Role in the Conflict. This first section demonstrates why conflict is always a two-way street. Consciously or unconsciously, we tend to assign full blame to the other party with whom we're in conflict, relinquishing our role in the dynamic.[iii] In this section, I'll instruct you to look deeply at *your* role in the conflict in your life and to identify the relationship dynamics that are causing you the most anguish. I'll also invite you to think carefully about your goal for a given relationship when in conflict and to consider what you truly stand to gain from

trying to "win" an argument. This section will further illuminate how powerfully our habitual ways of thinking and acting
can shape our interactions.[iv] By mindfully paying attention and
making small changes to habitual thought patterns and behaviors, you will find that you can spend less time arguing and
more time enjoying your relationships.

Part II: The Emotional Story. Once you gain awareness of
your role in conflict and an understanding of how it might
be beneficial to restructure your habits, I'll take you further
inward and teach you how to listen in a way that will help
you achieve better outcomes. Specifically, this section will
cover how to listen for what you are actually arguing over—or
the *why* versus the *what* in conflict. I will also stress the all-
important need to be aware of your inner narrative. Only by
carefully listening to the underlying source of our reactions
can we begin to figure out what's really motivating us. At the
same time, you'll learn to genuinely listen to what the other
person is saying and to ask questions designed to develop a
true understanding of their position. You'll be encouraged to
take the time to fully process what you're hearing rather than
immediately reacting to how it makes you feel. Calling upon
the self-knowledge and habits gained in Part I, you'll be able to
temper your reaction to conflict and stay open to the deeper
meaning underlying each party's words and actions.

Part III: Shelving Heated Conversations. This third section
will help you bring your more mindful inner behavior into

alignment with your outer behavior. By shelving or pausing when conversations and relationships become heated, you will radically alter the outcomes both in your own behavior and in your relationships. Making space to think and emotionally settle before reacting will help you identify the words and actions that will elicit more of what you want out of interactions. Even if you're the only one engaging in this process, you'll become less defensive and will learn to create firmer boundaries in addition to learning behavioral shifts that will prove vital in changing how you respond to others, from negative to neutral and even positive.

Part IV: Yes, You Can Get Along. Even despite your best efforts in enthusiastically adopting the practices described in the first three sections, deeply entrenched conflict may still flourish. This section invites you to strategize how to go deeper by getting vulnerable with your vision of any particular relationship, whether it is with another person or more importantly, with yourself. I will teach you strategies to prepare for future conflict by taking a step backward before moving forward. I'll stress how it's possible to get more of what you want out of all your relationships by embracing your vulnerabilities and visualizing your goals, thereby bringing them into reality.

This final section will also address the reality that the YES Method is an ongoing process. Compromise, concessions, and allowances are necessary in all our interactions.

The ultimate goal is for you to get the most out of your relationships and interactions over time. Inner and outer alignment with a healthy dose of patience is key, as is recalling always that as long as we remain open, our relationships are always evolving.

Rather than avoiding most difficult or uncomfortable conversations, using the YES Method enables you to engage in more important interactions in a more productive way. In reality, the YES Method brings us a better way to handle conflict that allows for positive evolution in our relationships. We tend to think of conflict as bad or unhealthy. However, with the tools of the YES Method, even the most entrenched conflicts can become opportunities for not only interpersonal growth but incredible personal growth as well.

Conflict is part of life. There's simply no avoiding it. Relationship conflicts of any kind can make us feel sad and powerless, and they carry the potential to upend our lives. But conflict can also be a gift. It gives us a rare opportunity to build and deepen our connections with others. By learning the YES Method, we can meaningfully restructure and sustain our relationships in a world brimming with conflict. We cannot only resolve the greatest conflict in our lives, but also transform our relationships and reshape our lives from the inside out.

With the YES Method, you can free yourself from needless conflict and chart a better path forward. Once you master all the steps within, you'll move from confusion to clarity, from crisis to calm. One day at a time, one conversation at a time, you'll achieve emotional freedom from conflict.

PART I

Your Role
in the Conflict

This first step of the YES Method asks you to clarify your role in your conflict, especially the emotions, prejudices, and assumptions you bring to the table. Like it or not, we are almost always part of the problem in any conflict...and we're also the only part of the problem we can control. Without fully understanding our role in a conflict, our ability to recalibrate the relationship dynamics is limited, and we may well miss out on opportunities for personal and interpersonal growth. This first step of the YES Method will help you to establish the receptive mental state that will enable you to do the next step: start listening and accessing neutrality.

This pivotal opening section will teach you to identify how your words and actions are contributing to the conflict in your life, how to get clear on your goals for each of your difficult relationships, and how to recognize how your habits (that is, your habitual thoughts, attitudes, and actions) may be contributing to the conflict in your life. When we identify and understand these habits, we gain the ability to shape the responses we elicit from others, kickstarting meaningful changes in our relationships. Only by first noticing our part in the conflict can true communication unfold.

CHAPTER ONE
Recognize Your Role

I'm no stranger to conflict. Growing up in a loud Italian and Jewish family where nobody shies away from an argument taught me a thing or two about how to speak my mind, react, accommodate, and get what I want at a young age. By watching a fair degree of chaos around me, I also learned that each of us truly has the power to radically transform our dynamics by making small changes in how we communicate. It's often said that it takes two to argue—and while it often may seem like the other person is "causing" all the fighting, by taking a step back, it's pretty easy to see our role in the conflict. For instance, if you're in the habit of talking to your partner while playing games on your phone, your partner is likely to feel slighted and to respond by being short, distant, demanding, or needy. Over time, this seemingly innocuous habit can erode a relationship. Or if you stroll into the office at 10:00 a.m. and work until 9:00 p.m., but industry standard is an 8:00 a.m. to

5:00 p.m., don't be surprised when you get admonished, even though you're working longer than most.

If you want your relationships to be easier and to begin getting along better with others, recognizing your role in conflict is essential. Let's look at the common unconscious mistakes, assumptions, and trouble we create in our everyday relationships. Once we get clear on how we're causing negative responses, we can figure out how to begin changing our thoughts, words, and behaviors so that we can start to feel better from the inside out.

It's Not You, It's Me

When I met my husband Mitch, we got engaged very quickly. We had great chemistry; he was sweetly attentive, and after years of dating my fair share of New York City and suburban professionals, I found him to be disarmingly fresh with his Toyota Tacoma pickup truck, his love for fishing and hunting, and his PhD in bird biology. There was just one catch: he was a country boy, and I was a born-and-bred New Yorker. I was in my early thirties at the time and had been a bridesmaid fifteen times. In my mind, it was time to get married and have kids. I left my highly regarded legal clerkship, my friends, and my family to move to the country, following my bird biologist husband to start a family. I knew he made less money than I did, but only after I relocated did I realize that he traveled a lot for work and when he was at home, he spent significant time at the gym.

When Mitch announced that he was going to be taking a new job that would take him away from home even more, although I had misgivings, I rolled with it. I gave him permission to do what he pleased, telling him that he should pursue his calling. It seemed like the right choice, but I still felt deeply frustrated. Within a short time, I found myself disenchanted with my new life, given my financial pressure to supplement his income and my growing parenting obligations. Before long, Mitch got a promotion that took him away from the house about 25 percent of the time. When he came home from travels, he was anxious to make up for the time he missed when he was away; he wanted to go to the gym, to hunt (which, as a meat eater, was a hobby I felt like I should support), to cook meals, and to spend time with our three sons. I felt irritated, alone, and invisible. I couldn't wrap my head around why my doting, upbeat boyfriend had morphed into a husband who wasn't giving me the attention I so deeply desired. Over time, I felt increasingly resentful and powerless to change the situation.

But then, it hit me: all these years, I'd been complicit in our uneven dynamic. I felt I had none of Mitch's agency in my own life. I'd bent my life in whatever direction he needed to support his dreams, but what was I doing for myself? Very little. And whose fault was that? Only when I hit rock bottom in our relationship did I realize that I was part of the problem—and that the only way I could change my situation was if I started to think and act differently.

I started to encourage myself the same way I encouraged Mitch. Instead of blaming Mitch for my unhappiness, I began to reframe my life. I became more engaged in the world—as I'd been before we got married. I started taking care of my own needs outside the marriage and away from my children. I was always diligent about visiting friends out of town, but beyond that I was doing very little for myself. Once I started to push myself to work out, to do more *for me*, and to do more in the world—by actually writing my first book that I had been dreaming about for years—I started to feel better.

As for Mitch—much to my surprise, he rolled with it.

At first, each time I told him I was exercising my self-granted independence, I braced myself for the potential back-lash. But to my delight, there was very little. I quietly yet radically rebuilt my world. I'd wasted years of my life living with anger and blame, without realizing that by blaming my husband for *my* choices, I'd been part of the problem all along. Now, maybe he could have been more aware of my feelings of isolation or more cued into my emotional needs, but overall, Mitch wasn't being an ass during these difficult days. He was just living his life as he wished. It was my job to do the same. How many years did I waste arguing or obsessing over how miserable I was? Far too many.

All too often, when we get angry, we blame others for our dissatisfaction and tell ourselves a negative story—and then we either fight or flee.[i] However, it is our job to notice and get clear on our role in each of our troubled dynamics. This doesn't mean that the problems are all our fault; rather, it means that we are part of the dynamic. Once we are mindful, or aware, of our role in the dynamic, we have the power to reduce and even eliminate high conflict. If we change our thoughts, words, and actions, we will elicit a more positive reaction, and the relationship will begin to shift. This clarity that we are part of the problem is *essential* before we can do any of the other work of the YES Method. This is where we start to recognize our own role in our troubled dynamics and begin to develop the strategies that will allow us to be part of the solution.

#RelationshipGoals

Of course, not every relationship holds the same level of importance. There is a continuum or hierarchy of relative care that we have for our partners, relatives, friends, coworkers, classmates, neighbors, and even strangers. While we are biologically hardwired for connection, our relationship goals vary. Since Mitch and I are married, I was highly motivated to figure out a way to resolve the conflict I was feeling over our lifestyle differences and to find a solution that would work for our entire family. While the resolution of our conflicts would perhaps be different if we divorced, because we share children and a history I would still be highly motivated to find a way to be respectful of him and his ways of doing things that I may not share.

Consider how important a particular issue or disagreement is to you in the broader context of your relationship. Not all arguments can be worked through, and not every relationship matters to the same degree. But for the most part, our interactions can be handled in a neutral manner, if not positively. Before digging in too deeply into your role in any conflict, you may consider assessing the relative significance of the other person in your life. Only you know how much you care about any particular dynamic or what your relationship goals are. Your goal may be as simple as getting along with your mother during a two-hour visit or feeling at ease when you walk into work each day. The decision to address an issue will depend both on whether the relationship is important to you and how important the issue is to you.

How to determine the relative importance of your relationships depends on who the person is relative to you. The questions you would ask yourself about a parent or sibling are different from if you were considering a coworker or employer, and again distinct from those you would ask yourself about a friend or romantic partner.

For instance, if you are exploring your relationship with your romantic partner, the questions you will want to ask yourself are around how you make each other feel, including:

- Does each individual make the other feel like a better person?

- Do you share feelings?
- Do you accept each other for who you are?
- Do you communicate respectfully?
- Do you share goals and values?
- Do you trust each other?

Whereas if you are exploring your relationship with coworkers or a boss, before blowing up your relationship there, you may consider:

- How important is the job to you?
- What are your chances of obtaining alternative employment?
- Is moving between departments viable?
- Is there a neutral party or a human resources department who can facilitate a mediation?

And, if you are thinking about your relationships with friends, you may want to ask yourself:

- How important is their presence in your life (are you in business with them/is there a financial or legal reason you ought to consider if you have a fall-out with this person)?
- How much time do you spend with them?
- Do you make each other feel good about yourselves? Do you make each other better people?

- Are you honest with each other where it counts?
- Is this person a part of a larger social dynamic or group that could be disrupted if you cut ties with them?

The bottom line is that each of our relationships is highly nuanced and needs to be carefully tended to before blowing up an important relationship or digging in too deeply with people who just don't deserve expensive real estate in our minds.

How we communicate with others can determine the outcome of an interaction, and to some degree, it may be worth the extra effort whether or not a particular relationship is especially important in an obvious way. As the previous questions might reveal, even if you don't care for someone or have an obvious need to maintain a relationship, sometimes there are secondary benefits of keeping the peace, as described in the section "Don't Cut Them Out, Cut Them In (Sometimes)" on page 20.

For instance, seeing eye to eye with your neighbor on political issues may not be as essential (or possible) as it is to reach an agreement with your ex about how often the kids should eat sweets at each other's homes. Think long term when assessing the relative importance of a particular dynamic. Set a clear, concise goal for each interaction. From there, you can build forward. In other words, rather than saying something global like: "I want to get along with my mother," try on: "I will have a pleasant visit with my mother today from 1:00 p.m. to 3:00 p.m." Small and specific baby steps are the only way to make big, lasting changes.

Not all relationships are created equal, but a sense of peace in your everyday life is essential. When you are feeling ill at ease in a particular dynamic, it's bad for your overall well-being. Whether relating to a stranger on the street, a condescending boss, or a disappointing friend, your relationship with yourself is impacted by your sense of peace with the world around you.[ii] You are free to dismiss the relationships that are no longer serving you in any way, of course. But before tossing too many of them, let's take a moment to look at how we contribute to the demise of our relationships and consider whether we can tolerate something other than the all-or-nothing approach to connection. The first step in making any meaningful change in a relationship is understanding what your goals for the relationship are. Once you are clear on your vision, you can set your new dynamic in motion.

Sometimes therapy is necessary to work through problems. The YES Method is certainly not intended to replace the important work that a mental health professional can provide. And unfortunately, some relationships are unsalvageable. If you are in a dangerous, abusive, or unstable situation, sometimes getting out of the relationship (long-term shelving!) is the only answer.

Clarifying Goals and Expectations: Find Solutions in Shades of Gray

When we're caught in an argument loop, we become single-mindedly polarized in our thinking. We delude ourselves into believing that if we get our way (to go on the vacation we want, host the holiday we prefer, do the project we covet), things will be perfect. In truth, conflict resolution is not black and white; the fact is that the best solutions reside in shades of gray. In order to tackle interpersonal conflict, you must do two things:

1. Get clear on your role in the conflict.
2. Clarify your goals for the relationship impacted by this conflict.

First, ask yourself how you may be contributing to the argument. How might you take greater responsibility in creating a better outcome for your relationship and for yourself? Ask yourself if there is something you may be able to respond to differently to improve the flow of communication. I have found that trying on replies or solutions that feel entirely foreign to how I instinctually react does something to loosen how I am thinking and creates opportunity for outcomes that I may not otherwise have considered.

Sometimes upon reflection, you may notice that you're more invested in simply being *right* than in the actual outcome of the argument. If that is the case, try on alternate responses to the upsetting issue or event.

In my role as mediator, I always hear two perspectives of the same set of facts. A point that strikes me as particularly interesting is that even the most polarized parties come into our sessions earnestly saying that they simply want whatever is "fair." But there is no such thing as objectively fair; all there is… is perspective. The rainbow may not lead to the pot of gold— the total win—but through deep understanding of perspective, we can make subtle changes to our thoughts, words, and actions—leading to a just-as-magical sense of ease.

Whether at home, at work, or anywhere else in life, it's all too easy for disagreements to spin out of control, which brings us to the second point: clarifying goals and expectations.

I see this all the time at the mediation table: when we're in a seemingly intractable argument, it's easy to get led down countless rabbit holes that only intensify the argument and feelings of distress and disgruntlement. For this reason, I find it particularly helpful to set out concrete goals right from the start. That way, when things go off track (which they inevitably will), I'm able to redirect the parties and their lawyers back to the resolution of these goals.

For example, in a divorce situation, the parties will often come into negotiation sharing that they have the common goal of sharing equal custody of the kids. But then, as we start getting into the details of the parenting plan, especially when young children are involved, often one of the parents may begin to insist that they should have most of the parenting time because the other parent is not adequately taking the children's safety concerns seriously enough. Rather than getting into a finger-pointing debate, we circle back to the previously defined common goal. Then, the position of needing to be with the kids "most of the time" is more likely to de-escalate by building safeguards (i.e., guns in safe, pool gate closed, agreed-upon bedtimes) on each side to ameliorate any concerns. Just a little baby step redirecting the parties back to the common goal of being equal parents refocuses the conversation in a positive direction.

When I am involved in a particularly complex or contentious divorce case, each side tries to get my ear. Sometimes, before I even sit down at the mediation table, they do their best try to convince me that the opposing party is completely responsible for all that is wrong in their world. They want me to think the other party is the sole cause of the conflict who singlehandedly broke down the relationship and to take their side from an emotional point of view. But I know from twenty-five years of practice that the way to resolution is from a place of impartiality. The first step of my work with clients becomes straightforward: to help them escape their attachment to being "right," and to get clear on what they truly want out of the mediation. It's the same for each of us in our everyday interactions.

Personality is in the Eye of the Beholder

Like my mediation clients, you probably have your own share of low-key troublesome people to downright difficult people in your life, whether they're specific people or certain situations. In today's world of extreme polarity, we need to learn to coexist with all the asses in our lives as if our lives depended on it. Because they do. And it all starts with acknowledging that from the perspective of the person or party with whom you're in conflict, *you* may be the problem and not even know it.

Back when the TV show *Friends* was still airing, guys I was dating often compared me to both the free-spirited Phoebe and the tightly wound Monica. When Guy Type A had a glimpse of my more whimsical Phoebe side, he greeted it with something other than elation. Similarly, when Guy Type B experienced my more uptight Monica traits, he didn't appreciate that part of me. Quite naturally, I saw myself as a fully integrated, balanced person, so when I was confronted with these extreme mirrors, I felt misunderstood. Rather than react defensively, I grew curious. What I came to notice over time is that different people perceived me with a hyper focus on particular characteristics—and the particular characteristics they focused on were those they didn't like. Personality is in the eye of the beholder.

If you were to ask two of your closest friends who are the most different from each other to describe you, you'll likely encounter the same outcome. Your friends would each list your qualities that resonate for them (or push their buttons) and overlook the rest. Similarly, if you were to ask a casual acquaintance to describe you, that person might focus on

aspects of your personality you didn't even realize you pos-
sessed. **How we see ourselves has little to do with how we're
experienced by others.**

Not everyone is going to see us and interpret what we do
in a positive light, and that's fine. The fact that we disagree is
not the problem—the problem is our failing to recognize that
whenever we experience conflict in our lives, we have a choice
as to how to think, speak, and act within it.

Just because we're part of the problem doesn't mean we're
doing anything wrong. Simply being ourselves could be the
conflict trigger within certain relationships. Maybe it's our
constant joke-cracking or ultra-serious manner that's an issue
for another person. Maybe it's our brashness, or shyness, or
how we think, look, or walk that's the issue. But regardless of
what ignites the conflict, it's what we do amid the discord—
especially how we think about our role in it—that empowers
us to successfully deal with the asses in our lives.

When you look at the conflict landscape in your life, it's
essential that you consider and even list the various ways you
could be contributing to the conflict. Because as tough as it
can be to admit it, we are almost always part of the problem. We can't effectively learn and practice the YES Method
unless we relinquish our belief that the other party is solely
to blame.

Getting clear on the fact that you're seen differently by
different people is powerful. By understanding how your

behavior is impacting those around you, you can both understand the limitations of certain interactions and make changes that will make the most important relationships work more smoothly.

For instance, you may find a colleague, Joe, to be disinterested and negative, but then overhear another coworker, Sylvie, using words such as "inspiring and engaging" when talking about him. Neither of you are necessarily crazy or lying. Rather, you have different perceptions. Now imagine that instead of Joe being perceived in totally different ways by different people, it is likely that your personality is impacting the way the colleague is relating to you. Maybe Joe knows you see him as condescending and exhausting to listen to, and so maybe he has decided to tune you out when you speak. Recognizing that the way you see things is not objectively "true" paves the way to begin reframing your perception, which will then likely result in different responses. A great tip to understand why people act differently than you do begins with understanding that their perceptions guide how they act and how they respond to how you are acting.

When we begin to explore how others see the world, we can start to truly appreciate how we may be seen by others as well as how we can better connect with people who hold different world views.

Let's look at various conflictual situations and open our eyes to the ways we're part of the conflict equation.

Don't Believe Everything You Think

Sometimes we become so attached to our positions that we jump to erroneous conclusions, creating loads of unneeded chaos. There are hundreds of ways this happens across all areas of our lives. Here's a simple illustration of what I mean:

I remember one Christmas, I told my brother I wanted to "do the stockings" for our collective five children. But before I could say another word, my brother dismissively said that he didn't believe in all the consumerism. I *may* have called him a bit of a Grinch or Scrooge and told him he was full of baloney, and then we turned our conversations to other topics. Normally he and I speak almost daily, but I think I can safely say that this Christmas stocking convo left us both a little irritated. The phones rang silent as we were each holding erroneous ideas about what was motivating the other. After about a week of neither of us reaching out to each other, one of us lifted the phone, and we finally took the time to get each other's full story. In his mind, he was assuming that I was going to load him with the annoying task of putting each stocking together. But had he let me finish, he would have understood that all I wanted to say was that regardless of who was going to take care of getting the stockings done, I just wanted all our kids to be together on Christmas morning so that they could open the stockings together. No more and no less. As far as I was concerned, how the stockings would be filled and by whom was still open for discussion.

When we cut off a conversation because of an assumed

response from the other person, we are cutting off the chance of having any meaningful two-way communication. Personally, I know I'm often onto the next thing before the speaker (usually my husband) has finished his thought. If I'm not paying attention, I can react or acquiesce to something before he's gotten to his main point. And then what happens next? He reacts, and I'm annoyed.

The Trouble with Pot Stirring

Let me give you a recent example from a former client of mine that will may sound familiar to you.

Lisa, a woman in her fifties, posted on her Facebook page that she was concerned, and a bit offended that many of the proliferating "Karen" memes (featuring the popular depiction of "a Karen" as a middle-aged, entitled, and ignorant white woman with an asymmetrical bob asking to speak to the manager[iii]) were anti-woman.

A thoughtful discussion ensued in the comments, until her longtime friend and colleague, Darren, made a casually insulting comment about aggressive women in the thread.

Lisa felt publicly shamed by her long-term friend. She'd deleted the post but felt that the friendship with Darren was probably over. She hadn't spoken to Darren at all beyond the exchange on Facebook other than a casual hello at work, and she wasn't sure if she ever would again. She was sad, but also enraged. *How dare he?*

In reading this, notice where your mind goes. Do you find yourself critical of Darren? Of Lisa? Of this very situation? Our fuses are shorter and less tolerant than ever. Navigating relationships at home and at work are hard enough, but navigating conflict online is often harder. Those interactions are at a physical distance, and they naturally lack the rich nuance we get from an in-person or even phone conversation. We are terrible listeners.[iv] Our failure to listen well impedes our ability to be the best communicators. On the online sphere, there is even a higher likelihood of misunderstandings without the benefits of body language, tone, and context.

Thankfully both Lisa and Darren retreated and did not further inflame the fire. Had either Lisa or Darren reacted emotionally to each other, this interaction could have caused the entire relationship to unravel. One reactive comment could have stirred the already bubbling emotional pot and disrupted a lifelong friendship. After some time passed, they had a difficult but respectful and ultimately productive conversation. Darren apologized for attacking people in the thread and Lisa owned that if she is going to post something controversial, she needed to accept potential criticism.

Don't Cut Them Out, Cut Them In (Sometimes)

What if you want your kid to have more homework and your kid's beloved teacher believes homework causes anxiety?

Or your mother-in-law is undermining the progress that you and your partner have made together in therapy? For many of us, the default reaction is to step away from that relationship, creating distance from the conflict. If that's often your approach, it's useful to consider that rather than cutting out the people who see things differently from how we do, sometimes the right solution is to cut them in—to engage them further in the situation and deepen their investment in the relationship and to strengthen the connections between you.

Let's look at Joseph, the sixteen-year-old son of my divorced clients Stu and Sophie. Joseph had recently been diagnosed with ADHD and was given prescription medication from his pediatrician. Stu and Sophie met with his therapist, Lucy, after the diagnosis. During their session, Lucy suggested to Stu and Sophie that she believed THC or marijuana was a preferable treatment for Joseph over prescription medication. During the same session, Lucy explained that unless she had fears for Joseph's safety, because of the child's age and the laws in the state where they lived, Stu and Sophie would not be notified if Lucy learned that Joseph was using marijuana or other drugs due to the confidential doctor–patient relationship between her and Joseph. While Lucy's comments gave Stu and Sophie pause, they weren't that worried that Joseph would actually be using drugs. They also noticed that most importantly, Joseph appeared to be doing better in school and at home following several sessions with Lucy.

Three months later, Stu discovered a tin of THC edibles from the local dispensary in Joseph's top drawer. He called Sophie, and as they discussed Stu's discovery, they assumed Lucy had encouraged Joseph to use drugs, and they considered ending Joseph's treatment with her. But before they met with her, they called me to help them weigh out other options. With my assistance, they realized that rather than cutting out the cannabis-loving counselor whom their kid trusted, they should consider cutting her in. Cutting Lucy out could result in Joseph resenting them or refusing to engage with a new counselor. Plus, the strides Joseph had made in his treatment could be interrupted.

Stu and Sophie met with Lucy again to figure out the best path forward. During the meeting, they learned that Lucy had been merely voicing her general belief that natural drugs are sometimes better than doctor-prescribed medicine during that earlier session. She was surprised to hear that Joseph was using marijuana. In addition, she also clarified that she never intended to support marijuana use in lieu of doctor-prescribed medication. In the end, Lucy agreed to move forward with Joseph in support of his parents' position against him using marijuana. Because Stu and Sophie cut Lucy in, they were able to address Joseph's drug use and preserve the effective client–patient relationship.

In dealing with conflict in either our personal relationships or our professional alliances, we risk losing something big when we reactively cut people out. When you find yourself in a similar scenario where your natural instinct is to bail, arranging a meeting or productive conversation with the other party to reach an understanding is often the best way forward. If you're inclined to have a cynical perspective, think of it this way: by keeping your friends close, and your perceived enemies closer, you're more likely to make a difference in your world. By cutting people in, often you're more likely to achieve peaceful outcomes.

In your life, as in mine, you will reach various crossroads with people across home, work, online, in your extended family, and in your social circles. Clarifying how we're part of the problem and what we want to do about it is the first step of the YES Method. Only then we can decide how to move forward in the relationship.

Whatever the case in your life, remember that you cannot access the power of the YES until you've taken full ownership of your role in the conflict in your life.

Hillary and Simone Recognizing Their Roles

Hillary and Simone had been friends forever. They'd always been different from each other, but over the years they had mapped out a dance that worked for them dynamically...until it didn't. Their style and communication clash caused a break in their friendship.

Had both of them taken a step back and to assess how they were creating or adding to the conflict, their friendship may have had a chance to not only survive, but to thrive.

D.E.A.R. Exercise

When we feel heard, our emotional-defensive armor begins to release. This release makes it easier for us to see our own role in the conflict. In the previous sections, we delved into some common yet unintentional ways we could be participating in the problematic dynamics we have in our lives. Start off with this self-introspection exercise to help you gain some clarity independently. The entire exercise should take about fifteen minutes.

For this exercise, you will need a quiet place where you can be alone with your thoughts, a piece of paper (or a journal), and a pen. On your sheet, draw a table with four columns.

Label the columns Dynamics, Emotions, Actions/Reactions, and Revisit in the same order.

Then, pick a relationship with dynamics you aren't happy about. To prevent yourself from dwelling too long in a column, I have included a prescribed amount of time for you to fill in each part.

Dynamics

For three minutes, write down the dynamics that are bothering you. Focus on describing the aspects of your relationship that you aren't happy about. This could be:

- The other person's actions or words
- The way they do or say something
- A recurring argument
- A pattern of behavior or habit

It can be anything that the other person does, says, or causes that sets you off.

Emotions

For another three minutes, write down how you feel about it. This time, recall the emotions that are evoked by each dynamic you listed. Avoid name-calling; focus on your feelings. When you are done, take a minute to pause before you move on to the next step.

Actions/Reactions

For the next three minutes, write down your actions and reactions when dealing with the difficult dynamic. This is where you truly begin to look inward: focus on what *you* do during or after encountering the dynamics that are upsetting you. If you are having trouble remembering, consider asking yourself the following questions:

- Do you become defensive?
- Do you feel agitated in your body?
- Do you look at your cell phone while the other person is talking?
- Do you escalate the conflict with facial expressions?
- Do you refute or dismiss the other person's point of view?
- Do you jump to conclusions?
- Do you bring up issues from the past that have already been resolved?
- Do you introduce unrelated conflicts?
- Do you become loud or large, verbally or physically?
- Do you respond sarcastically or spitefully?
- Do you rehearse your response rather than listening to the other person?

What dynamics are bothering you? Write them down. Write down how you feel about it (no name-calling, same as in the "Emotions" column). Consider your actions and reactions when dealing with the difficult dynamic.

Once you are done, take two minutes to think of how the other person behaves during these interactions. You may write them down if you wish, but the goal here is to recall and consider how *your* behavior affects *them*.

Revisit

For the last three minutes, write down alternative ways you think may create a positive, neutral, or even a less negative response by altering your actions and reactions when dealing with the difficult dynamic.

It can be as small or as big as you'd like. Remember that whatever you list doesn't necessarily have to be your next course of action; the goal in this part is to simply explore other ways of being that you may not have considered, especially when you are in the heat of the moment.

If this is the first time you are trying this exercise, it might be easier to choose a relationship that isn't too personal; for example, a coworker or a friend who isn't particularly close to you. Sometimes, it is more difficult to be objective when we are too emotionally invested in the other person or the situation,[v] so practicing with a relationship that you can distance yourself from can be a good way to dip your toes before diving in.

These exercises are best done when you are calm and collected, as a peaceful mind can give way to more objectivity as you recall and review your reactions;[vi] however, as you will learn in the following chapters, you can also return to this exercise when you are taking a pause from a heated conversation.

Consider alternative ways you may create a positive, neutral, or even less negative response by altering your actions and reactions when dealing with the difficult dynamic.

And last, while this may feel silly, it will get your creative juices flowing and may elicit better outcomes moving forward as you take ownership of your role in the dynamic.

KEY TAKEAWAYS

- Getting real with yourself on how you are contributing to conflict—consciously or unconsciously—is the first step in improving your relationships. We have agency not just to help resolve conflicts but also not to throw fuel on the fire and unintentionally make things worse.

- You must decide how important each relationship is to you beyond the present, conflict-charged moment. Our role in a conflict will inevitably shift depending on whether it's with a stranger, friend, parent, or spouse. Understanding the importance of the relationship affects one's priorities and goals and it is key to navigating conflict smartly and skillfully.

- Ask yourself if you are pot stirring, making assumptions, cutting people out unnecessarily, or failing to communicate gently. From someone else's perspective, are you the "difficult person"?

CHAPTER TWO
Harness Your Habits

Nancy, an attractive, successful mother of two, was forever feeling left out of other people's social plans. She could count the number of weddings she'd been invited to and was painfully aware of all the social events where her name didn't make the guest list. She just could not understand what she was doing wrong. In her mind, she was a great host and had made great efforts over the years to introduce her friends to one another. Adding emotional upset, on more than one occasion, the friends that she'd introduced to each other bonded so well with each other that Nancy fell off some dinner party invites in favor of the newly acquainted. Once, friends she'd introduced even went so far as to travel the country together without including Nancy in the plan. Nancy couldn't understand why this was happening to her. She felt like she was a good friend and that she did not deserve to be cast aside. She couldn't figure out what she was doing wrong or why nobody seemed to value her friendship.

It's possible that Nancy had bad luck or poor judgment in friends, but since many of these people remained close to one another through the years, maybe it was something else. Nancy's overall victim narrative didn't end at the dinner table. It crossed into her work life as well. She was consistently passed over for promotions and was seldom picked to be part of any important committee at her office. When it comes to interpersonal dynamics, Nancy consistently felt misunderstood and shafted.

Our attitude, or way of thinking about someone or something, is a primary determinant of how we think, feel and act. As we're exposed to stimuli over time, we form opinions, make evaluations, and develop attitudes that inform our habitual thoughts. Attitudes can be positive, negative, or neutral. The world gives us feedback based on the attitudes we express. In turn, our attitudes and thoughts impact our behavior or how we act. Checking in on what we are thinking is just as important as checking in on how we are acting; this applies to how we perceive ourselves and how we view ourselves in relation to others.

Whether we are talking about how we speak to ourselves or how we interact with others, whether we hang up the phone abruptly, work out, or stick to our diet, is all dictated by our automatic routine behavior. Nearly 40 percent of all the actions we take in a day are a result of habits rather than well-thought-out decisions.[i] Changing any of our habits takes sustained, intentional effort over time. Willpower, or self-directed neuro-plasticity, makes change possible. Many of the things we do are simply because of continual practice.

Because Nancy had the attitude that she was destined to be treated as "less than," it makes sense that she conveyed an air or attitude of insecurity and weakness. As long as she maintained that attitude, nothing would change. What's so amazing about Nancy's story is that in her middle age, Nancy decided she'd spent enough time living in self-doubt. She began to change her attitude toward herself and in her life. Working with a coach, she developed the habit of telling herself that she is good enough and deserving of respect, love, and even adoration. Even though it felt inauthentic at first, she expected more of the world around her. She began to communicate a stronger, more confident energy. At forty, Nancy started reconnecting with old friends and making new friends with untapped colleagues. She began feeling better about herself. Within a year, some of the old friends who had all but cut her out were inviting her to join them on some of their escapades. She also began to find greater success at work, surrounded by colleagues who showed her the same respect that her new life attitude demanded.

Nancy spent her retirement years surrounded by loved ones. By changing her habitual thoughts or attitudes about how she would be treated, Nancy felt less conflict and started to have more social and work-related success. In changing her mind-set about her relationship with the world around her, her life began to improve. Small shifts can create tremendous out-comes around us. Fake it 'til you make it.

Recalibrate Your Thinking to Reduce Conflict

In the previous chapter, we worked to get clear on your role in your interactions (positive and negative; conscious and unconscious), as well as your desired relationship goals. In order to begin to change any of your thoughts, words, and behaviors, you must embrace a paradigm shift in how you both look at and interact with the world, and in turn, how the world both sees and interacts with you. I had a friend I studied with in law school who used to tell me to "loosen my brain" when I was being rigid in my thinking. Though more than two decades have passed since we studied together, I often think of that phrase when I or someone with whom I am disagreeing could use a dose of flexibility. With a bit of mindful awareness, we can recalibrate our thinking.

Each time we repeat a behavior or thought pattern in response to a particular emotional trigger, we are reinforcing the association between the circumstance and our actions or thoughts. In order to create a truly massive, lasting change, we must make many tiny changes in our everyday behavior. Our behavior is the sum of all our habits, conscious and unconscious.

Habits run so much deeper than we think. They go well

beyond the habits of making our beds, flossing our teeth, and washing our hands. When you think about your "bad" habits, something tangible probably comes to mind, such as forgetting to turn the lights off, not picking up after yourself, or loading the dishwasher the "wrong" way according to your spouse. But habits also extend to our thinking, especially our ways of perceiving and interpreting the world around us. Experts have found that these perceptual habits are so deeply ingrained in us that they determine the structure of our days and how we process the world around us.[ii] Just like any other habit, these automatic behaviors can either serve or undermine us. While we may not be able to completely change our natural temperament, we do have the power to modify the habits we have developed over time.

Change Your Thinking in Three Steps

Step One: Notice your thoughts and actions.
Step Two: Consider the consequences or relationship goals.
Step Three: If you care, adjust your thoughts or actions.

In order to change our habits in a steadfast, lasting way, we need to first tweak our habitual behavioral and thought patterns. We addressed the first two steps in chapter 1.

You will recall that Step One emphasizes the importance of being aware of our thoughts and actions. Remember, only when we recognize and take responsibility for our part of the conflict (no matter if it's internal or external), can we decide whether we care about having a different outcome. When you are feeling caught in conflict, ask yourself what part you are playing.

Step Two requires us to decide whether we are happy with the consequences of our thoughts and actions. Is the way we are thinking or acting contributing to our sense of calm or inner peace? Is it allowing us to achieve the relationship goals we have in a particular situation? Is it aligned with our core values? If so, then we don't need to change a thing. But, if we realize that parts of our life are out of alignment because of our own thoughts or actions, it may be time to replace our thoughts or actions with something that matches the outcome we are looking to achieve.

Step Three is the step this chapter will address. It asks us to literally replace the thought or behavior that is not serving us with something more productive, with the goal of developing new pathways and habits that serve our goals in a positive way. For instance, if you are a nail biter, one way to change that habit is to do something different with your hands, such as interlocking your fingers together in the moment that the nail-biting impulse hits. Similarly, if you want to change your habitual thought patterns, you need something new to replace those old patterns.

While you may *want* to change the actions and habits of those around you, all you can really do is alter your response. The goal is to change your dynamic by literally restructuring your thoughts, words, and behaviors in response to their annoying behavior. For instance, when your husband absent-mindedly fills your tank with the diesel fuel, causing your car to be towed and hundreds of dollars of expense, rather than lashing out, consider sitting quietly and consider how he may feel having made such a mindless error. If your coworker has talked over you in a company meeting for the umpteenth time, rather than lashing out, consider how you can be more assertive in the conference room. Build forward from there. Remember, your task is to change your reaction, not their behavior. But, if you are clever, you may be able to accomplish both.

It can be especially difficult to make changes in our relationships when we don't understand how our habits are impacting outcomes. This is the case even when we already are getting along. When we're fighting with someone else, noticing our habits—both large and small—becomes that much more challenging. Conflict stirs up insecurity and noise in our mind that can cloud our judgment and cause us to go down emotional rabbit holes that only make the discord worse. The antidote to getting swept into the chaotic, conflict-driven swirl is to quiet our mind.

Practice Makes Permanent

How we do things on a day-to-day basis matters. I try to impart this wisdom to my teenage sons. Practice truly makes permanent. Repetition is the basis of all habits, good and bad. The more we do something a certain way, the easier or more automatic it becomes. Practicing something makes us better at doing something, especially when practice is done regularly. *How* we practice or do something matters. We are training our brains to process how to do things in a particular way.

The more we do something the wrong way, the more comfortable that behavior becomes. Once, I set up two friends to go on a date in New York City. The guy, John, is a hilarious person. He's an Ivy League–educated doctor and the son of two professionals. My girlfriend, Caitlin, was a banker. They met at an upscale bistro in Manhattan. After the date, I got a debrief from both of them. Though there was no love connection, John reported that he enjoyed his time with Caitlin. Caitlin's primary impression was that John was nice, but she commented to me that after eating, John picked up his plate and licked it. I couldn't believe my ears. Later, when speaking with John, I called him out for having such bad table manners and he incredulously broke out laughing, stating that his mother was always reprimanding him for this very behavior. He was shocked that he did this in public. After many years of casually sopping up the food on his plate with his tongue at home, he did the exact same thing at a fancy restaurant. The behavior was so automatic he didn't even remember doing it. Old habits die hard.

The same thing happens in our interpersonal relationships. If you're getting in trouble at work for not meeting deadlines, consider identifying one behavior that is interfering with you meeting those deadlines. Rather than hoping for better out-comes next time, pick something small that you can do and do it every day. For instance, if you find yourself getting into senseless arguments with an otherwise beloved coworker over politics, refrain from having those conversations and instead engage in something less controversial. Rather than feeling angry and irritated by one another, you may find a common love for cooking or sports. Discipline yourself to exit senseless argument loops. And, do your best to talk about something agreeable. Do this every single day. Over time, your impulse to engage in this dysfunctional debate subsides.

Inner Quieting

Inner quieting is the state of mind where your thoughts stop claiming or co-opting your attention.[iii] It's a state of inner strength, peace, and calm. This slowing down of restless thought or activity can create space to transform discord into harmony. The secret to inner quieting when you're triggered is in noticing how you are feeling in that moment of upset. Only by inner quieting can we truly focus on the issues that matter and address the conflict sensibly. The act of noticing requires you to be aware of what is happening in your body and then to slow it down. I realize how impossibly aspirational that may sound, but it's something we can all do—and it can be a game changer in helping us to notice where we are about to go awry in our reactions. A great, accessible way to quiet your mind is to simply find a place to sit and breathe, with eyes gently closed, for ten long deep breaths in and out while reciting a simple calming positive affirmation.

When I am feeling reactive, I find a place to briefly sit, close my eyes, and take ten slow breaths while telling myself with each undulating breath, "I am radiantly calm." I know that while this exercise may not transform you into a completely different person, the simple exercise of shutting down the moment's chaos and replacing it with a simple, positive statement can make all the difference in your ability to quiet your mind and begin to notice what is happening from various angles. Throughout the book, I will introduce a variety of meditation techniques. Meditation is incredibly helpful in managing conflict. If this technique isn't working for you, perhaps one of the others will.

If "I am radiantly calm" doesn't work for you, find a statement that is better suited to how you speak to yourself. While this process is not going to change your basic personality or total response to whatever is going on around you, it will give you the mental space to make better choices and to respond more intentionally. When you quiet your mind, you create the opportunity for better outcomes and greater understanding.

Outer Calming

We all have different sensibilities, and we're not all going to be one another's cup of tea. To get along better with others, it's really not essential that you change your entire way of thinking. We may like our attitudes and have no desire to change our global perspective on anything. You can be clear on your perspectives and thoughts, even rigidly so, and still change how you communicate, just a little bit. A small shift in your communication habits can make all the difference in your relationships.

Cal considers himself a liberal with socialist leanings. He is thirty-six years old and a professional. His older brother, Greg, completely disagrees with all of Cal's attitudes about basically everything political, both on the social side and on the economic side. The brothers are three years apart and were raised together by a single mother. Cal always looked up to Greg as a kid, and although they are very different people, they have always had a very strong bond.

Greg's family visited Cal's several times a year for long family weekends together. Cal and his family looked forward to these visits. But once Greg's family arrived, Cal's family couldn't wait for them to leave. As Cal's big brother, Greg felt that it was his job to show Cal the error in his ways of thinking. In Cal's children's presence, Greg would engage Cal in uncomfortable political debates. When Cal was immovable in his position, Greg would push back and even begin name-calling. While Cal was accustomed to his brother's style, it was a very uncomfortable dynamic for everyone else at the table. Greg seemed completely unaware of the discomfort that he was causing, even though his wife, Stephanie, and Cal both asked him to stop arguing. Eventually, the dinner invitations slowed down and when they came, Greg's family was expected to stay at a hotel rather than at Cal's home.

This left Greg confused and hurt. He didn't understand what had gone wrong. Greg was in a lifelong habit of telling his brother what to think...but this time, he had to consider what he needed to do to keep his brother in his life.

After some thought, Greg realized that did not have to change any of his political attitudes in order to have a good relationship with Cal. What needed shifting was his attitude about what made good dinner conversation. He needed to go cold turkey on the public political debates that no one wanted to hear. Limiting the content changed the conversation and relaxed the mood.

This family crisis opened the conversation between Greg and Stephanie, who expressed that she too disliked controversial dinner conversations. While Greg felt upset and hurt by both his wife and his brother, he also knew that he cared deeply about both of these relationships. Greg made a list of other topics he could discuss at dinner and practiced daily at home. He also called Cal and apologized for stirring up so much discomfort. The next time they all got together, dinner conversation was much more pleasant and this trickled down to a higher quality visit for everyone. One small, specific change practiced over time can make all the difference.

The Power of the Will (and Won't!)

After a year of her gym being closed during quarantine, Cici was feeling out of shape. She had always depended on exercise classes to get her physical activity. Now that this option was no longer there, she decided to commit to a daily walking routine. Just two daily half hour walks made all the difference in how she felt. Starting was hard, but by doing it each day, she established a habit—and after several weeks, she could hardly tolerate when something interfered with her three-mile jaunt. Cici's willpower to sustain her physical activity enabled her to develop a new habit that changed the way she behaved to match the goal she had in mind.

There's another type of power that's rarely discussed but equally important as willpower, and that's the power of the "won't." Rather than committing to engage in a particular behavior, you can decide to refrain from doing something.

Let's recall Cal and Greg's story from the previous section. Greg resisted changing his habit of bringing up controversial dinner conversations for a long time by telling himself (and others), "That's just how I am." But in fact, arguing at the table is a mutable behavior. Changing this habit did not require Greg to shift his political views or personality; it simply demanded that he change his attitude about what makes good dinner conversation. In this case, Greg is exercising the corollary to will power: *won't power*. Won't power is the commitment to *not* do something—to refrain from a behavior or to override that which is not serving us. We can simply determine that we will or won't do something in response to a certain trigger. By remembering the reactions that we've determined we will or won't have, we can commit to a simple change each time we encounter a triggering moment.

It's worth noting that Greg didn't just decide not to talk politics. He came up with a list of alternative topics of conversation as part of his plan to get along better. Sometimes it's easier to substitute a positive behavior than it is to stop a negative one. The example of the person who tries not to think about the elephant in the room and can therefore think of nothing but the elephant comes to mind.

It can be challenging to take on new ways of being, especially when a habit is deeply ingrained from childhood. For example, maybe you grew up in a home where insults were frequent and rapid. What if you are in the bad habit of telling your sons that they "run like a girl" or you notice that when you are irritated with someone you reflexively call them the "R" word. You know you shouldn't say these things, but over your lifetime, you've developed this bad habit. You have casually held onto these expressions as part of your everyday vernacular. When you're called on it, you may feel defensive and gripe, "You can't say anything these days." If you don't mind cutting off conversation and alienating people at best, and being fired from a job or losing respect of loved ones at worst, then continue using sloppy and offensive language. But if blurting out insults and slurs truly does not comport with your core values, rather than holding onto old-school bravado around these offensive statements "not meaning anything," maybe it's time to change. An old dog sometimes can learn new tricks. Consider embracing your "won't power" and find less offensive and more descriptive ways to express frustration with a person or situation.

Instead of saying something derogatory when you are frustrated, perhaps consider incorporating a reserved smile or even intentional nonresponse. Your choice to say nothing is also a strong action that speaks volumes, especially to an audience that is accustomed to being frustrated with your typical brash way of communicating.

One Small Change

We tend to revert to old habits because they are so ingrained in our subconscious. We can feel like we are literally combating inertia when we take on something new. And this is why it's important to take baby steps—to notice, assess, and recalibrate your habits one at a time. By repetitively inserting one small habit change into each of the areas of your life that is causing you conflict, you will develop new habits that can transform how you feel and how you interact with others. And once you notice how your reflexive behavioral habits are impacting your well-being, you can forge forward with new ways of being.

For instance, let's look at what happens whenever you encounter something undesirable your spouse or partner does, such as leaving the toilet seat up or forgetting to lock the front door. You may be in the habit of telling yourself how inconsiderate or thoughtless they are whenever they do such a thing. In fact, it could be that they're just oblivious or distracted, so perhaps mild frustration is a more warranted response rather than boiling outrage. Recognizing or noticing your habitual ways of thinking about conflict can be game-changing in recalibrating your relationships and in mitigating conflicts. Once you notice your habit of thinking, you will then unlock the ability to change your habitual ways of communicating. You may be able to prevent future conflict by behaving as though the annoying action (or inaction) was an accident, even if it wasn't.

The good news is that with small shifts in our thoughts and behavior, we can change our habits and positively impact our relationships. By changing our actions, responses, and reactions, we impact the people and environment around us. The first step is to notice your own thoughts and resulting behaviors in response to a situation. When you notice a habit that is not serving you, you can change it. Habits are automatic thoughts and behaviors that grow over time. And they're hard (but not impossible) to break.

Once you recognize your unhelpful habits, you can have the power to change them by imagining how you would optimally respond to a situation and then implementing one small shift at a time. For instance, as shown in the previous example, if you find yourself in an irritated loop with your spouse, you can improve your relationship by addressing one element of the habit loop at a time. You do this by (1) recognizing the reactive habit that is not serving you (feeling angry and blowing up at your husband the next time you see him); (2) stating your goal reaction (disimpassioned or no reaction); and (3) recalibrating your response. For instance, rather than blowing up at him and then retaliating with some punishing behavior, you simply cross-check your emotional response to the behavior with the relative importance of the particular transgression.

To do this, you will need to first engage in inner quieting. Next, change your habit of thinking about the behavior. And last, change your behavioral response. If your goal is to get along better, consider reframing your perspective. Rather than allowing your emotional response to ignite an argument, maybe you release your attachment to the behavior you are looking for—change your habit of thinking. Or maybe, you find a gentler way of discussing your desired outcome by agreeing to take on something that you do that irritates them—change your habit of communicating or behaving. He puts down the toilet seat; you shut the lights when you leave the room. You shut off the lights for several weeks, and then gently remind him to put the toilet seat down. Or, you do both because maybe you decide it's not worth the argument. Problem solved. The purpose of this exercise is to illustrate that you too can sit calmly and create a list of alternatives that best suit your situation.

The notion of changing an ingrained behavior may sound

unrealistic, but the steps in this chapter will make it doable. The main thing to remember is to take baby steps. Large transformation happens in small bits at a time, and before this change can be observed from the outside, a big part of the work must be handled on the inside. Internal change is of foremost importance. Remember, adjusting our habits is all about changing our own reactions, not controlling the other person's behavior.

The Power of Specificity

Before leaving the topic of habit, I need to underscore that in order to make habits lasting, we need to name our new goal with specificity. Amorphous words of intention are unlikely to result in any real goal actualization.

For example, for years, I've noticed that in January, it's harder to get a parking space at the gym than it is any other time of year. The culprit is the ever-popular New Year's resolution to "lose weight" or "get in shape." My momentary aggravation with all the new gym-goers is quelled by the knowledge that easy parking is just a few weeks away. That's because about 80 percent of all New Year's resolutions fail.[iv] The trouble with New Year's resolutions is that usually, they call for broad, sweeping behavioral change without setting up enough infrastructure. Deciding "to lose weight" or "to get in shape" requires more moxie than most of us can summon all at once— and it's not a very well-defined goal. What we are really asking for is a total shift in inner consciousness—overnight.

While New Year's resolutions may last for a few weeks, they're unlikely to stand the test of time. That's because it's nearly impossible to make global stretches beyond the habitual comfort zone in a big way over a sustained period. In no time at all, most of the cars will be back tidily in their garages each morning...and parking for my car and space for my yoga mat will once again be easy-peasy.

When New Year's resolutions are generalized wishes to become a different person (happier, healthier, stronger, wealthier), failure is all but inevitable. When you do not articulate specific intent, the outcome tends to be based more on chance. And, while the absence of a specific goal may enable you to feel like you have more easily kept your resolution, whatever you achieve is likely to feel less satisfying.[v] Clarity in exactly what you wish to do differently or to achieve allows you to actually execute your goals. When we set ambiguous benchmarks for ourselves, we put ourselves on course to accomplish nothing in particular. Without a clear goalpost, our commitment to whatever vague goal we're aiming to achieve will more likely ebb and flow. When we ask of ourselves to make one specific change, commitment to making that change is easier to sustain. Over time, we are no longer thinking about this concrete, specific behavioral change as a task or chore, even if it was at first. It becomes automatic, or a habit.

The trick is to make the resolution specific and clear. Rather than creating the global change of "losing weight" or "to exercise regularly," promise yourself something more specific. For instance, the resolutions to "eat sugary desserts no more than twice a week" or "to walk at least a half hour a day" are more likely to create a lasting behavioral shift. The difference is that you are not asking yourself to completely abandon your entire identity. Rather, you're taking on one clearly articulated change at a time. Once this new behavior is integrated into your habit, you can add a second small goal, and then a third, and so on. Over time, you will achieve the global vision of "being healthy."

In my professional life, I spent many years arguing with myself about how to best manage my mediation practice. I knew I would be much more efficient if I were to take on a team to get many of my tasks accomplished. But when I thought about hiring and training a team (the nonspecific goal of "being a manager"), I felt overwhelmed, so I did nothing at all for a long time. One day it occurred to me that this team did not have to spring up all at once. I could begin building a team by taking on one part-time employee.

This leap of faith was scary to begin with, but it was the best money I ever spent. At first, I questioned my ability to delegate efficiently, or to trust someone else to do tasks for me after so many years of handling everything on my own. But in record time I went from hiring one part-time assistant to building a small, reliable, trustworthy team to take things off my plate and bring my business to another level. This experience helped prove to me that by implementing specific changes in our responses to certain triggers, we have the ability to powerfully calm the conflict and change how we feel.

Hillary and Simone

Let's think back to the story of Hillary and Simone and their salon. Hillary knew she was a people pleaser. But never had she considered that on the micro level, this meant that she was in the habit of reflexively agreeing with others, even when she didn't really mean what she was saying. She was so concerned with making people happy in the moment that she hadn't considered the long-term impact both on her relationship with Simone and with how she felt about herself in concert with the world around her. Though it was hard for her to acknowledge, Hillary recognized that the constant need to please left her often feeling in the one-down position in her relationships with others. Had Hillary realized that she had this habit, she could have been transparent about it with Simone and that relationship could have both been more honest and potentially may have lasted longer. Plus, going forward, as a baby step, Hillary could have committed to a new pattern of behavior where she would substitute "Let me think about that" or "I'm not sure that's going to work for me" each time she felt herself inclined to say "Yes" when she wasn't really feeling it.

This concept of making one small change applies both to our relationships with others and to our relationship with ourselves. Some conflicts are purely internal. We debate with ourselves over ways that our lives could be better, calmer, or more exciting. We criticize ourselves for our perceived failures. We question ourselves at every turn. Other conflicts may be instigated by other people, and yet, we always have the ability to shape our dynamics so that they are less confrontational. The trick is to build new ways of thinking and responding to all the input that comes our way. Once you recognize how you are contributing to a conflict in your life, you can then quiet or calm your inner emotional reactivity so that you are able to take the steps needed for a habitual lasting change.

Bringing it Together

Changing our habits and attitudes in interpersonal relationships is usually complicated and layered. If your situation feels overwhelming, give yourself permission to tackle it one piece at a time.

Mitch and I used to argue quite a lot about my insistence that our boys study musical instruments. When my eldest was just starting to study violin, my husband did not understand why we had to practice every day. He found the ritual an imposition on our already busy life. We were in constant unpleasant conflict over the practicing.

To make matters worse, for months, maybe even a year, other than squeaking out the Twinkle variations, all we worked on every single day was the position of my son's pinky and thumb. Another violin teacher may have allowed him to whisk through the pieces without first establishing the hand position, but not Emily. She was known to be the best teacher, hands down. And she was highly demanding and relentless in her expectations from her students. To begin with, she was singularly focused on building a lasting habit or routine that would carry forward for years to come.

I wished she would ease up a bit and teach more songs. And I wanted my husband to take on enforcing half of the practicing time. However, he wanted no part of it. I was so frustrated with the whole situation that I began to catastrophize in my mind. But then I realized: I was not going to change Emily or Mitch.

Instead, I decided to change my attitude toward both the teacher's demands as well as my husband's reluctance to engage with our son's violin practice. In order to change my attitude, I needed to create new habits for myself. First, I needed to get out of my routine of asking or expecting Mitch to help with this activity. Each time I had the impulse to ask for help, I replaced my habit of feeling frustrated and angry at Mitch with the affirmation to myself, which was "I get deep satisfaction watching my son develop his concentration and musical ability." Mitch and I stopped fighting about the practices, and we both started to enjoy the concerts.

Next, I needed to stop wishing Emily would go through the pieces faster. She was teaching my son the value of practicing a small habit to create small change that would ultimately enable him to be a more proficient musician. Emily knew what she was doing, and I was letting my own impatience get the better of me. My desire to move along quickly was my issue, not hers. I used the same affirmation ("I trust Emily's process") each time I had the impulse to push back on any of the practice requirements from the teacher. For years, my son and I practiced tiny technical details required by his teacher together, and as a result, he was later able to quickly learn challenging pieces. Through Emily's attention to small change over time, I learned a powerful lesson that small changes build upon each other. She was establishing the foundation.

This is the same way we succeed when instead of saying, "I am not going to argue with my ex anymore" we say, "I am not going to contradict my ex when he says x, y, z (thing of inconsequential importance that I usually make a stink over)." Once we drop that negative part of our dynamic, it is easier to begin to develop positive momentum.

The repetitive attention to this tiny detail of intentionally engaging in affirmative self-talk was foundational to my son's later success. One small change. A shift in attitude. Practice makes permanent.

Writing Exercise: Bringing it Together

1. Think of the relationship dynamic you want to improve and identify your "bad" habit or the behavior you want to improve. (Look back on the previous exercises and pick one.)

2. First, write down what triggers your "bad" habit. ("When I am not selected for an advancement at work, I feel like a victim.")

3. Next, write down how you respond to the trigger. This is the behavior you want to change. ("When this happens, I withdraw and engage in extensive negative self-talk.")

4. Now is when you recalibrate how you want to change. Write down how you would like to respond or behave instead. ("Instead of looping in negativity, I will patiently remind myself of the things I excel at and will engage in activities that uplift my sense of self-worth.")

KEY TAKEAWAYS

- Our role in each conflict is informed by our habits—
  habits of attitude, thoughts, and behavior. These
  result in unconscious actions (or inactions) that fuel our
  conflict.
- Getting clear on our habits can vastly improve our relationships. By just noticing our habitual thoughts, actions,
  and reactions, we can increase our self-awareness and
  create space for alternative habits. As we begin to
  change our unhelpful habits, we start to actively reduce
  the conflict in our lives.
- Engaging with techniques such as inner quieting and
  outer calming will help you track your triggers and
  observe your own reactions. You can recalibrate habitual
  thinking in three simple steps:
  - Notice your thoughts and actions.
  - Consider the consequences or relationship goals.
  - If you care, adjust your thoughts and actions.
- Tapping into your will power or won't power can help
  you change your patterns of thought or behavior, one
  small, intentional change at a time. Adjusting your
  thoughts and actions may take time, so be patient with
  yourself and remember that practice makes permanent.

PART II

The Emotional Story

Now that you understand how you may be contributing to conflict and how to define your relationship goals and you've begun taking steps to change your mental habits, you will be able to leverage this newfound mindfulness to listen for what is actually happening within and around you during conflict. In order for you to know how you are actually contributing to any negative dynamic—and in order for you to keep your fingers on the pulse and understand what habits may be forming and creating conflict—you need to learn to listen beyond the noise and focus on hearing what's really happening beneath the surface of whatever situation you're in.

In this section, I will teach you how to engage in active listening in order to open the neutral space of your mind and begin to distinguish interests from positions. Harnessing the habits you learned from Part I, you will begin to cultivate new listening habits of hearing—both your own true interests and the interests of the other party.

CHAPTER THREE
Neutrality Is the Portal to Possibility

Back when my boys were little, they were in constant motion. I spent years deliriously exhausted keeping them safe from running into traffic and from inadvertently harming one another with their constant horseplay. Mitch was traveling for work a lot of the time and while he was away, the fantasy of having co-parent reinforcement was intoxicating. I imagined he'd swoop in and relieve my constant sense of responsibility, and I would get a break. But in reality, it wasn't actually easier when he was home. He was tired from traveling and needed time to regroup. Instead of calmly backing me up as I imagined, he responded to my requests more slowly than I wanted, and when he was engaged with the boys, I often didn't agree with his parenting style.

While I'd dreamed of a small break in the nonstop parenting responsibility, what I got felt like more chaos and the admonishment that I needed to "parent" more. We were completely at odds. Not only did our interaction often whip up more chaos for the kids, we created and amped up our own layers of disagreement. We were both trying our best to get our kids from point A to point B, but we were also pointing fingers at each other while feeling like we were failing miserably at controlling our unruly boys.

We were able to transcend this dynamic once we began to hear where we each were coming from. Mitch was reactive because he was feeling anxious and a little embarrassed that our kids were misbehaving. I felt frustrated by what felt like an unwarranted attack from the parent who was not around much of the time. I was reactive because of my own defensiveness and insecurity that maybe I was not doing everything "just right." By each owning our side, we were able to depersonalize what felt like unwarranted attacks. It was only in retrospect that we realized we each needed to take a step back and understand what was going on for one another so that we could get our co-parenting skills on track—together.

Today, when similar problems arise, we're more mindful about how we handle things. I am more intentional about articulating my expectations earlier so that he has more time to process, while Mitch has become more open to discussing things before they blow up. But intellectually understanding that we are part of the problem is the easy part. Deciphering the specific thoughts and behaviors adding to the conflict and then figuring out what to do about them is something else. It's easy to analyze when we're feeling calm and rational, but it's hard to do so when we're smack dab in the middle of the conflict. When we're in the heat of the moment, we're not thinking clearly; and whether we realize it or not, we tend to be so emotionally flooded or overwhelmed by our feelings that we become unable to see our side of the problem. When we're in this defended state, the instinct is to go into fight or flight mode, which neither addresses the issue nor serves us internally. Instead, we must take the physical and emotional space to regulate so that we can think through the issue and respond calmly. By learning to self-regulate and respond more slowly when things get heated, we can better discern when to lean in and when to walk away. We can avoid the pitfall of focusing on external causes of conflict. Blaming the other party may leave us feeling triumphant in the moment, but it does nothing to make the conflict better—leaving us feeling frustrated and powerless as a result.

When you feel your temperature start to rise, here are some potential responses to use before lashing out:

- "I am feeling stuck in blaming you. Let me think this through and get back to you."
- "I appreciate that we have different points of view. Maybe we can discuss this later when we have both calmed down."

- "I hear that you're frustrated/angry/irritated (hearing/ seeing the other person's perspective)."
- "I know that I am not listening to your point of view right now. Maybe we can take turns listening to each other?"
- "I hear you. I will think about that."
- "I know I am not perfect. Let's talk about this together with HR/a mediator/therapist."

In all of these cases, you are literally making space to calm down your system, to slow down your reactivity and to allow the other person opportunity for expression. This small conversational shift creates opportunity for large relational change.

In order to process all sides of a conflict, we must listen from a place of neutrality. By "neutrality," I mean reaching a mind-set that has no attachment to a position or a side. When we reach neutrality, our response systems (or emotional brains) relax and our thinking brains are free to engage. Neutrality leaves us open to listening for all possibilities and allows our curiosity about the other party to unfurl. With curiosity and an open mind, we enter a space where we're able to calmly listen and intentionally respond to others rather than simply react. This is the space we need to inhabit in order to pivot our approach to conflict and position ourselves to untangle previously unsolvable problems.

In my worst moments, I was reacting to Mitch's communication style: his actions, inactions, his tone of voice, and the pace at which he communicated (which was slowly). In my mind, every little thing that he did or didn't do—as long as it failed to match my exact expectations—was an affront to my person. It took me a long time to truly understand that Mitch wasn't purposefully antagonizing me. I was emotionally flooded at that time and feeling like he was being aggressive on purpose. I was unable to regulate my thoughts and reactions in a way that helped anything. Instead, I added to the chaos by engaging in moments that could have been ignored, and by ignoring issues that could have been better addressed.

I realized over many years of clumsy and painful interactions that my husband was just a different kind of communicator than I was, and nothing I could do was going to make him operate at my speed. Once I had accepted this, I found that to make the communication less painful, my goal shifted to being able to slow down, take a calming breath, and listen more. By entering a more neutral space, I was able to respond to the situation from a more objective perspective. I realized that the key to prevent my emotions from controlling the situation was to step out of my own shoes for a moment (which was especially difficult in the middle of a heated argument) and regulate my thoughts and reactions so that I could observe from a more objective perspective.

A vital part of achieving emotional freedom from conflict is listening not just to what is being said, but also what is unsaid: patterns of speech, body language, tone, etcetera. It may seem simple enough to be mindful of these nonverbal communica- tion cues, but it is easy to confuse being resentfully reactive and neutrally perceptive. In both cases you may pay close attention to what is said and left unsaid, but the difference lies in your mind-set. You need the neutral mind-set in order to perceive not only what is being communicated, but also the underlying intention. The goal is to access a neutral perspective so that you can distinguish between your emotional state and the speaker's intent in the hopes of resolving a previously troubled situation, and in so doing, be able to take a rational and objective course of action.

In this chapter, you will learn to listen for—and access—the neutral space between two disparate states of mind or positions, and you will see that you can skillfully start to navigate conflict and feel better sooner.

Interestingly, in the context of high-conflict situations, I've noticed that sometimes navigating disputes online can be easier than doing so in person. I think that this is because there are fewer gestures or facial expressions perceived—the words or intention can be the focus rather than the more subtle antagonistic ingredients that tend to cause emotional stir. Simple interaction with words alone sometime can actually lead to more efficacious conflict resolution.

The Secret to Finding Solutions

Rhonda and Bill split after seventeen years of marriage. Rhonda found Bill irritatingly slow and ineffectual, and Bill accused Rhonda of always having to get her way. The fact is that they were both kind of right. Rhonda knew her own mind, and Bill was more inclined to be agreeable and then resent his choices, most of which he felt had been thrust upon him by the sheer power of Rhonda's will. Thankfully, they were able to resolve their differences in mediation, but they still had two kids to finish raising. They lived in a small town and neither of them wished to have their reputation besmirched by the other.

With some distance from one another, Rhonda noticed the things she had appreciated about Bill: his down-to-earth sensibilities, trustworthiness, and commitment to their children. Although she very much wanted the divorce, with retrospect, she did recognize the goodness in his intentions, even if he hadn't been a perfect fit for her.

On the other hand, left to his own devices, Bill realized that Rhonda had filled his life with adventure and opportunity that he would never provide for himself. He also realized how easy she'd made juggling the kids and her work responsibilities appear.

It is a little ironic and maybe a bit of a shame, but after years of finger-pointing and hard feelings throughout the course of their marriage, Bill and Rhonda finally learned to embrace neutrality through their divorce. As their separation created the physical and temporal space they needed to take a step back from their troubled dynamics, and as they shifted their attitudes with the help of mediation, it quickly became clear to Bill and Rhonda that the only palatable road forward included them each accepting each other, personalities and all. Finally, they were able to embrace neutrality.

I have a hunch that had Rhonda and Bill made some space in their hearts for their mutual differences while they were still married, their relationship may not have deteriorated. But even though they wound up getting divorced, they each feel like their marriage and their family was a success, even though it did not last a lifetime.

Even if we don't care about being liked by everyone, most of us want to generally get along with others and live in harmony.[i] We want to go to bed at night feeling that we were cooperative, or at the very least, that we aren't going around doing just whatever we please without regard to the feelings of those around us. Like Bill, we don't want to feel pushed around; like Rhonda, we want our clearly communicated reasonable desires to be respected. What I have discovered in over two decades of mediating is that we can all get more of what we want...if we listen better. The trouble is that all too often, we are too positional in how we approach our differences. Getting stuck in what we want limits the possibility of considering the range of best outcomes or solutions. Accessing neutrality means considering a wider range of possibilities, rather than the yes-no or right-wrong binary thinking that we're all prone to when we're feeling triggered.

I used to call my grandmother and ask how she was doing. She would often say, "You know, the usual—many worries, few problems." I think her answer is illuminating for many of us. When we fixate on an issue or worry about something, we often catastrophize the situation. By accessing neutrality, we can create a space to see the difference between free-floating anxiety (i.e., vague worries about the future) and real problems that require our full attention and swift action. When we consider our concerns through a more neutral perspective, we can avoid catastrophizing whatever situation might lie before us.

A great way to think about neutrality is to recall how you thought about things when you were a kid. There's this great bit on *Brain Games*[ii] (a show I've watched too many times with my nine-year-old son) that illustrates this point perfectly. In this bit, groups of adults and children are shown similar amorphous, Rorschach-looking images and asked to describe what they see. Almost uniformly, the adults described the exact same thing. In contrast, the children came back with a wide variety of responses reflective of their naturally open and creative way of being. After being shown the children's results, the adults were asked to look at another image and to try something else. This second time, the participants were asked to pay attention to, or "listen for," their childlike open-mindedness. Their resulting answers were diverse and even funny. When adults were encouraged to go beyond their limited thinking about what was "correct" and embrace a broader range of possibilities, they were able to embrace the same sort of neutral space that can be so helpful when navigating conflict.

Finding the "Just Right" Option

Psychologists such as Jeremy Shapiro have referred to the solution to binary thinking as the "Goldilocks Principle."[iii] A great way to find what's "just right" in our personal development is by reverting to neutral. To get neutral, we need to take a momentary pause from speaking, writing, and reacting, and open our minds and hearts to hear what the other side is trying to say. This kind of neutralized thinking will enable all but the most zealous advocates of a position to begin to make space to see things in a less adversarial way.

Sometimes listening requires us to simply observe our thoughts and listen to the messages we are gleaning from them. For instance, when your mother calls you for the umpteenth time in a row with the same list of obsessive worries, you may have the impulse to avoid or even to block her calls, to yell at her, or even to cry because you just can't take it anymore.

When we're feeling provoked we make stressed induced decisions.[iv] Even the most open-minded of us tend toward polarized thinking when we're upset. We get fixed in binary paradigms and miss important opportunities for connection, growth, and conversation. We fail to see all the possibilities that are before us.

The next time your loving but exhausting mother calls with a list of concerns, your tendency might be to either avoid the interaction by blocking her calls or cutting her off before even saying hello on the one hand or to engage too much and finish the call feeling upset and dreading the next interaction on the other. We fail to recognize that there's another option. Recognizing the other person's need can go a long way to reaching resolution. In this example, it may mean that your mother has a need to voice her worry, and you may have a need to not be bombarded by her constantly. There is a way to get both of your needs met and avoid hurt feelings and agitation. To figure out the need, step back from the emotionality of feeling attacked (or bombarded) and ask yourself what is going on for you. Maybe you feel mistrusted, interrupted, or simply annoyed. By recognizing that your mother has another need (maybe to be needed!), you can skillfully create a path forward that meets both of your needs. In this case, maybe you can plan a thoughtful conversation with a preemptive cure-all laid out before the next time she calls. Rather than waiting for her to call you, you can call her and request that she save up all of her worries for one call each week where you promise to just listen for an hour. This would help to diminish the constant deluge of neurosis directed at you. And you remind her how grateful you are to have her, and how much you love her. (With any luck, this approach will work as well for you as it did for me and my mom!)

No matter what kind of conflict we are dealing with, interpersonally or within ourselves, we need to find the just-right option and manage our emotions in order to do that. When we manage our emotions, we are better listeners and better communicators. We can pay more detailed attention to body language, subtext, intentions, and back stories to arrive at a better understanding both of ourselves and of those around us.

Writing Exercise to Find the "Just Right" Solution

A great way to find the "just right" option is to write down the things you really need from whatever situation you are grappling with. On a sheet of paper or in your journal, write down the following at the top:

1. The situation that is bothering you
2. How you feel about the situation
3. Your ideal solution

Now it is time to dissect your "ideal solution." Below the description you've just written, draw two columns.

In the first column, write down the parts of your ideal solution that you have no control over. Get creative and write down everything you can think of that is external to you. Acknowledging the things you cannot change can be very liberating.

In the second column, write down the parts of your ideal solution that you can control. Here you will list everything that is within your power to change.

With these two parts of your "ideal solution" laid out, you can begin to analyze alternative ways that you can deal with your less-than-ideal situation. To begin, look at the first column. Ask yourself:

- How integral is this aspect in the execution of your ideal solution?
- Is there anything you can do to gain control of this aspect?
- If someone else is in charge of this aspect, are they someone who is willing to collaborate or compromise?
- How feasible is it for you to gain control of this aspect?

For the second column, consider:

- How would the things on this list affect the overall situation?
- Are there any other options that can help you improve your situation that aren't dependent on column 1?

Here's an example of how this exercise might work:

Let's say that you are handling a demanding boss who is constantly throwing new tasks at you before you've completed the last one. In this case, maybe what is upsetting you is that you're frustrated that you can't seem to get ahead on your big project with the ever-growing to-do list.

Your feelings are that you're out of control, over-extended, stressed, unappreciated, or disorganized.

Ideally, you would receive your work in smaller chunks, and you would be appreciated for a job well done after each task.

While you may be able to ask your boss to give you a list of what is most important to handle, you are unlikely to change their style of delegating work. However, you can create your own workflow system so that you have a sense of accomplishment each day. In this example, let's say you have one large project and then a constant flow of requests you are also expected to handle. Rather than tending to all the smaller requests and shirking your responsibility on the larger project, designate three hours a day to the large project regardless of what else is being handed to you, and spend the other five hours attending to the projects and issues of the hour. By considering what you need to create your own just-right circumstances, you will greatly diminish your frustration and overwhelm. If necessary, you may communicate to your boss that you have put some thought into how best to balance your workload and explain the system. He or she may have a different hierarchy of tasks that they wish, and letting them know that you are thinking things through may help make this conversation more useful. Added bonus: your boss may be impressed that you have thought it through so carefully to optimize your performance as an employee!

The thing to remember is that your mother who is calling you and your boss who is inundating you are unlikely to be intentionally annoying, frustrating, or overwhelming you. Rather, they are managing their needs—maybe even their own neuroses and disorganization with their own skills. Even if your worldview from childhood leads you to believe you lack agency in your life, this is the moment where you dismiss this mistaken belief. You are the master of your environment and of your experience. And it is your job and your job alone to create your just-right experience, regardless of the cards your present circumstances have dealt. If you find this unimaginable, you may need assistance to explore your self-limiting beliefs.

I once heard a story about someone who grew up in a country where people's career paths were determined by how they scored on a test at a fairly young age. When the time came for him to receive his fate, he was granted a career path that diverged from what he had desired in his young, hardworking, and lofty, dreaming heart. I found this story shocking, given my experience of having the privilege and worldview that I could decide who and what I wanted to become. He explained that even though he wasn't assigned the exact career path he'd dreamed of, he came to realize that by exploring all his options, there was a way to make this assigned fate interesting. The gift of that limiting environment was that it inspired him at a young age to always find the just-right angle, to work the edges and to transcend the disappointment by creating a fulfilling career, even under this imperfect situation.

All too often, when we feel victimized by our circumstances

or are stuck in an unpleasant or displeasing interaction, we blame others for our circumstances. Often, we say things we don't mean; but that doesn't mean we're liars. We're people pleasers, we're not paying attention, we meant what we said in the moment; we're lazy, and we're sloppy. The list goes on and on, and in the end and we're all responsible for a lot of messy relationships. But it doesn't have to be that way. No matter what kind of conflict we are dealing with, interpersonally or within ourselves, when we manage our emotions we can find the "just-right" solution to whatever obstacle we're facing. When we manage our emotions we have the power to slow down and we're way more likely to communicate effectively and to have better outcomes.

I'm Listening, You're Not Listening, and Other Lies We Tell Ourselves

By failing to actively listen, we can become clumsy, blamey, and often slightly heated in conflict situations. There's a difference, of course, between listening for what is unsaid and making unsubstantiated assumptions about what other people mean. Active listening requires us to go beyond just hearing the words, but it provides opportunity for better communication.

If there's one thing I am an expert in, it's dealing with argumentative people. I fancy myself a chief peacekeeper and often say that while I suck at many things, I am great at resolving the most complex disputes in mediation. And yet, in some circumstances in my own life, I am just as guilty of not listening and reacting as though something has been said, or not said, or even thought, as anyone. Let me give you an example.

When I was a baby lawyer, I was so frustrated with the winner-take-all, scorched-earth mind-set embodied by so many of my beloved colleagues that I caused myself a lot of unnecessary grief. When I was involved in divorce cases that did not involve abuse of any kind (domestic or financial), I was relentless in my attempts to get the other side to negotiate and to see the case from a holistic perspective—even when that was literally the opposite of what I should have been doing if I wanted to "win" in court and have way less mental aggravation. I was so busy passionately explaining why it was important not to cause collateral damage to the children and why the family unit mattered even after it was split that I failed to listen to what the other lawyer was saying. I heard the words, "Yes, let's work this out," but I didn't look or listen for the subtext: "... after we go through all the legal hoops" or "...after we bill six figures" or "...after we have an appropriate show in front of the judge."

I just assumed that my perspective was the *only* perspective; because of this, I failed to hear that opposing counsel might have a different approach. It was only when I realized that the agenda of my colleagues varied from my own that my frustration level decreased. In the end, the vast majority of my cases resolved at the negotiation table, but getting there was more emotionally exhausting to me than was necessary. In many cases, I believed I understood what the case needed to be resolved, but I wasn't really listening. I had my agenda of creating a peaceful, conflict-free exit for the parties, but by remaining single-mindedly focused on bringing my opposing counsel to the negotiating table, I created more conflict rather than less.

Listening better necessitates "getting neutral" and recognizing that unconscious biases or patterns develop in marriages and other long-term relationships;[v] one person might say, "I don't care," and the other person might lose their mind because they "know" they are being set up to make the "wrong" decision, which will later be thrown back in their face. When we are open to neutrality, we are able to hear with a broader tonal frame. In retrospect, I realize that as a young lawyer dealing with highly contentious opponents, I had the strong unconscious bias that they were making our cases more difficult than they needed to be because they were aggressive jerks. Over a lifetime, I realized that was a ridiculous and simplistically biased viewpoint. In fact, most litigators believe with all their heart that they are simply zealously advocating and preventing some wrong from befalling their victimized client—and in most cases, they probably are.

Neutrality doesn't just open us up to other points of view; it also helps us look at conflict in the proper perspective. At the end of the day, in my case at work, the backstory didn't matter.

What mattered is that I recognized that there is more than one way to approach a divorce. Some people think it's all about the money. Some people think it's all about the relationship. By bridging this gap, and developing a deeper understanding of all the nuances of what matters in a divorce, I was able to both develop a stronger muscle of no longer viewing the process as one-size-fits-all; and more importantly, I was able to gain much greater respect and admiration for my colleagues who approach their cases differently than I do.

Active Listening Exercise

A great way to start understanding why you're really arguing and to move through and beyond conflict is to is to engage in an exercise called "active listening." Active listening builds trust with the speaker so that you can better understand the issues and diffuse conflict. It can also help you increase your knowledge and understanding of whatever issue is in discussion. Active listening allows each person to be heard, thus increasing understanding by the listener and diminishing the need for the speaker to engage in endless repetition and often curtailing the instinct to be right.

This exercise is ideally accomplished with two engaged participants, with each taking turns listening and then reflecting.

Here's how it works:

The parties agree on a set amount of time that you will each get to speak. During that time, the designated speaker will state how he or she feels about a particular topic in a short sentence. It is important to use only feeling words rather than derisive terms. So, rather than saying, "I feel like you are a jerk," the listener may say something more like, "I feel disrespected." After calmly reflecting back what the speaker says the listener asks, "Is there more?"

Let's say, for example, that the parties agreed to five minutes per person. When the time starts, the speaker says, "When you leave the toilet seat up, I feel disrespected." Then the listener says, "When I leave the toilet seat up, you feel disrespected. Is there more?"

Then the speaker lists something else, "When you give me a long to-do list, I feel overwhelmed." The listener would then reply, "When I give you a long to-do list, you feel overwhelmed. Is there more?"

The speakers keep going back and forth until the five minutes have passed and then they switch roles. It is important to note that the goal of this exercise is to promote a neutral tone of voice and to practice having a calm, metered approach to conversing over even the most difficult topics. This simple exercise fosters the creation of an environment of neutrality and opens the conversation to more creative, efficacious outcomes.

Aside from creating a space for us to address our issues from a neutral standpoint, this exercise also allows us to be more in touch with our emotions, and further raise our awareness of how we react to stimuli. This is not an avenue to "attack" the other person—directly or indirectly. Notice the speaker does not say, "I feel like you're out of your mind/clueless/useless," or call the long to-do list "rambling" or "outrageous."

Active Listening in the Wild

Once you have developed the ability to be an active listener, you can employ this strategy to make a difficult interaction easier. To be an active listener you must pay attention, withhold judgment, reflect back the speaker's statement, clarify, and summarize. The goal is for the speaker to experience the sense that you, the listener, have been empathetic to their perspective. That you truly hear their pain and understand what they're going through. Notice that you do not need to agree with anything the speaker is saying; you simply need to listen and hear their perspective without interjecting your points of view.

Sometimes, however, the tone of voice, the way a person is speaking to you, or their body language is enough to set off a heated dynamic. People may express themselves passively (or nonassertively) or aggressively (or assertively). Although we tend to be tone-deaf to our own styles of speaking, of course we can also be neutral, positive, and negative. Further complicating things, we respond depending upon what our natural or nurtured tone happens to be. We react to various tones with our own signature style—which can make a situation better or worse depending on style compatibility. Consider both the tone of the speaker as well as your own. Sometimes, asking yourself how you may come across may be better than taking into account who the listener is. Remember, communicating is not one-size-fits-all, but active listening is a great start for most.

Hillary and Simone Getting Neutral

After Hillary delayed signing the second lease for their salon, Simone felt personally affronted. From her perspective, Hillary was being passive aggressive and not acting like a good friend. Rather than listening for Hillary's point of view, Simone shut down. And even though there wasn't any obvious betrayal, this failure to communicate feelings resulted in the ending of a lifelong relationship. Simone understood that she was an ambitious and intense person, but she never considered how her style may have inadvertently silenced Hillary. And, even if ultimately parting ways as business partners made sense, if they had taken the time to understand one another's emotions around where they each envisioned the salon over the next five years, they may have been able to part as friends.

While it may have been a push to get Hillary to own her fear around confrontation or for Simone to recognize that her drive and ambitions were buttressed by a deep sense of fear that she would never be as successful financially as she dreamed, it could have gone so differently. They each could have simply neutrally acknowledged that they each understood that the other had feelings about their respective careers that were no longer complementary to co-owning a business. Simply reflecting that they each understood that they valued and respected each other even though they did not understand where the other was coming from could have been enough to save their important relationship.

An Exercise to Improve Emotional Vocabulary

As a quick exercise you can do by yourself, try taking five minutes to say how you feel when a certain thing happens—see if you can fill the time by only describing your emotions. Believe it or not, many of us do not have access to words of emotion. You can find excellent "feeling wheels" available online. Examples of some emotion words that may be used to express feelings of upset are: angry, confused, depressed or sad, fearful, hurt, lonely, remorseful, or inadequate. Active listening can of course also be used as a tool to express appreciation.

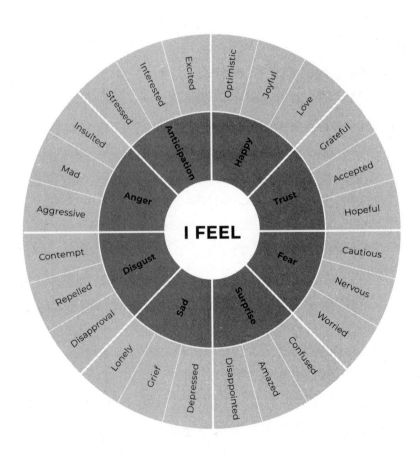

For example, if your partner takes care of your usual job and makes the bed, consider saying, "When you make the bed in the morning, it makes me feel respected/appreciated/loved." This can be particularly helpful in a dynamic where someone complains that they feel invisible, underappreciated, unseen, or lonely (all examples of feelings words). Examples of emotion words that may be used to express positive feelings are: joyful, happy, appreciative, calm, amused, pleased, thrilled, elated, or attached.

Writing Exercise for Active Listening

First, if you are trying to hear your own emotions, this is a great time to get out a journal and start writing. On one side of the page, write down the trigger such as: *when this happens...* or *when I do this...*

Directly across from the trigger, write down how you feel. Read it back to yourself. Then, just beneath it, note the trigger in a neutral way and note your feelings in a neutral way. Soak that in as well. Recognize that you have the power to begin to transform how you feel just by beginning to practice thinking about your experience in a different light.

Here's what I did literally a year ago:

When my sons are yelling at each other over nonsense I feel enraged.

I notice my sons are yelling at each other. I notice I am feeling upset.

Then I soaked in the feeling of neutral space between what was happening with my emotions and judgment versus what was happening factually. My response to the situation, absent judgment (i.e., over nonsense) and emotion enabled me to listen to each boy without reaction and de-escalate the situation.

Reconsidering Conflict

Opening the neutral space in our mind toward all potential outcomes dismantles the all-or-nothing thinking that interferes with positive interaction. Rather than viewing a conflict from the zero-sum-game outlook, listening neutrally informs the listener that there may be a different and equally harmless story at play. When dealing with others, another great way to open this neutral space is to ask yourself to consider:

1. Other reasonable explanations
2. Best alternative outcomes
3. Worst alternative outcomes

We all have stories in our minds that feel true, but our perspectives can vary tremendously from those of the people we interact with. While each of our stories may be based on facts, they're also infused with mood, context, and perspective. So, by exploring the other reasonable explanations, we can avoid unnecessary hurt. When we consider the container of probable outcomes through the lens of the best alternative outcomes and worst alternative outcomes, taking a position of compromise will probably seem more palatable. It becomes easier to arrive at practical solutions.

Other Reasonable Explanations

I have a friend, Tanya, who was interested in learning about buying a particular piece of real estate from a friend's husband, Chuck. When she approached him at a party and brought up the subject, he abruptly cut off their conversation. Tanya left the party confused and upset. She had been sure he would help her, but in the wake of his curtness, Tanya assumed that Chuck thought her questions were stupid and that he must hate her.

I advised Tanya to consider other reasonable explanations for Chuck's behavior, especially explanations that took her out of the equation entirely. Maybe he'd lost a loved one earlier that week and found himself at a party feeling anything but social. Maybe he didn't want to talk about work at the party. Maybe he was also interested in the property and felt uncomfortable discussing it with her. Maybe he had been caught cheating, and he and his wife had a policy that he couldn't talk to other women. After going through all the other reasonable explanations, Tanya's anguish dissolved as she realized she couldn't possibly learn the real reason for his inexplicable behavior. She accessed a neutral mind-set toward the situation: "Chuck is struggling with issues that have nothing to do with me or with the real estate I am asking him about. I am open to the possibility of alternative reasons, and I accept that I may never learn any of them. I release any expectation of response from Chuck."

Best and Worst Alternative Outcomes

When navigating a conflict or negotiating a resolution to a problem, we always need to carefully consider what's at risk. Especially when we feel backed against a wall to make a decision, it is absolutely essential to understand all potential outcomes. Only by considering the best alternative outcomes and worst alternative outcomes can we make our most well-reasoned decision and pick a path to move forward. First, Tanya considered the best alternative outcome (that Chuck would call her in a day or two to explore possibilities about the property) and the worst alternative outcome (that Chuck would never call her and his wife would also ice her out without explanation). Tanya created a range of probable outcomes across the best to worst continuum. Then, there was nothing for her to do other than wait and see how Chuck would respond to her request. Tanya was able to enjoy her evening and remain calm for the next few days, after which Chuck did in fact call her and ultimately broker the deal on her behalf.

In forcing ourselves to engage in these inquiries, we are making space to open our minds to hear what's really going on for us both in this issue and in our lives.

Writing Exercise to Create Space for Alternative Outcomes

A similar exercise to the one we did for neutral listening can be particularly useful if you find yourself caught in a yes/no paradigm. In your journal, make three columns. In the first, write down what you're arguing about. In the second column, write down what you want to happen ideally. And finally, in column three, write down the reasons you want what you want. This exercise will begin to loosen up the space to create the possibility for alternative outcomes. (The process will be explored further in chapter 4.)

Let's say you moved away from home for your partner's job when you married, and you really want to be home every year on Christmas with your aunts, uncles, and cousins. But your spouse wants to have quiet Christmas mornings at home. Although you're typically flexible, in this one argument you feel very strongly that you can't budge; you feel like they're being argumentative for the sake of it. It's not like they even want to go see family, and to you staying home on Christmas feels like a punishment. This argument will tend to become a polarized conversation that ultimately may upend the holiday season not just for you, but for your children. You can create the space to see what is going on underneath the conversation. You will begin to notice the neutral space start to open and possibilities unfold.

What we're arguing about	My ideal outcome	Why I want what I want
I want to go to with my family, my partner wants to stay home (alone with the kids).	We will be with my family at Christmas, and my partner will be content with that outcome.	I feel lonely. I am afraid I will lose my connection to my extended family. I believe extended family is essential for a sense of belongingness, community understanding and for societal well-being.

Working through this exercise on your own can be very useful, and if you can get your partner to engage in this process, this three-part inquiry can also help you begin listening to and maybe even understand where your partner is coming from. For example, rather than deciding that they're being argumentative and tit-for-tat, consider other reasonable explanations. Maybe they're just trying to satisfy their own childhood fantasy. It could be that as a kid all they ever wanted was a quiet family Christmas, but their siblings wouldn't participate or a family member would invoke chaos through their drinking. Maybe their desire to stay home has nothing to do with what you want and everything to do with a core desire of their own. Next, take a look at the best alternative outcome and worst alternative outcome if you dig in your heels on insisting that you have every Christmas with your extended family and none of them at home. The best alternative outcome is maybe that your partner adjusts to what you want and you have the perfect holiday with happy loving people all around you. The worst alternative outcome may be that they decide you're so uncaring and selfish that they don't want to be married to you anymore and after you split you only get to have your kids half of the Christmas holidays.

When we are neutral, we can listen for the full range of alternative reasonable explanations and the best and worst outcomes for both sides. When we begin to notice our thoughts and infuse some space around them, that is where we avoid making assumptions and open ourselves to listen for other ways of being and thinking. Therefore, when we access neutrality, we are far more likely to achieve optimal outcomes since our interactions with others become more fluid and accepting. Getting neutral gives you the gift of space to hear the full range of possibilities.

With this open mind you are now open to consider other reasonable explanations and unpack the range of outcomes (best and worst alternatives). Through this exercise, you create opportunity for greater understanding and more wholehearted outcomes.

KEY TAKEAWAYS

- A vital part of achieving emotional freedom from conflict is listening not to just what is being said, but also what is unsaid: patterns of speech, habits, tone, etc. The point is not to project certain beliefs onto our friends and colleagues, but rather to slow down and observe the situation from a more objective or neutral perspective.

- You can invite a calm conversation and access neutrality by maintaining a calm tone of voice and by engaging in active listening practices to neutralize any conflict.

- Getting caught in a yes-no paradigm limits your opportunities to reach a balanced solution to your issues. Using the writing exercises for neutral listening and alternative explanations and outcomes can help you open your mind and consider choices beyond the black-and-white thinking that most of us can be trapped in.

- Before catastrophizing a situation, consider other reasonable explanations for a particular behavior or action.

Making a list of alternative explanations that are equally sensible and more palatable will enable you to start to shift your thinking. This will assist you in reconsidering the explanations you are spinning on without judgment.

- Before acting or reacting, try active listening and consider the following questions:
- What is the *best* alternative outcome to the solution I am considering?
- What is the *worst* alternative outcome to the solution I am considering?

When the best and worst alternative outcomes are each explored, you will have given yourself the range or container in which to create your best probable outcome.

- It's difficult—and, frankly, probably impossible—to approach every conflict with absolute neutrality. But the more we're able to open that neutral space, training ourselves through such exercises, the more neutral—and thus the more clear-headed and even-keeled—we can become.

CHAPTER FOUR
The "What" versus the "Why"

Back when I was clerking in divorce court, I was expected to resolve the most high-conflict, deeply entrenched cases so that the court was less burdened and the litigants could save their energy and money. I was young, and at first managing the litigation seemed like a Herculean task. But what I figured out in short order is that most of the time, if I named the emotions in the room (i.e., enraged, frustrated, worried, etc.) the issues would melt away, and it was almost like the cases resolved themselves.

In one of my most memorable cases, I had clients who were arguing about child custody and who would keep the house. One of the reasons that Joe and Rita were divorcing was because Joe had cheated on Rita. While this fact was a crucial factor in their decision to divorce, it was not legally significant in terms of outcome; in litigation, who cheated on whom did not have any bearing on how assets were to be divided. I point this out because during our meetings, the fact that Joe had cheated on Rita kept on tangentially entering the conversation. Joe continually rolled his eyes and half-heartedly apologized or denied her allegations. Round and round they went—Joe and Rita were caught in a senseless argument loop about something that ultimately would not affect the outcome of their divorce from a legal standpoint.

After listening to Rita cry and describe her experience for an hour, I realized she needed to be heard.[i] The bold thirty-year-old me said something like, "It sounds like it feels like your life was a lie." And then swiftly, I turned to Joe and validated him by saying, "Just to clarify—I do not think it was a lie. I am just acknowledging Rita's feelings about it." Rita then cried that "nothing is fair!"

Like magic, as I reflected her feelings—that she just needed to know that she would be okay, and that she would have a nice place to live with the kids without giving up her right to part of Joe's pension—she was able to settle. We hit on the why, and then the case moved.

I realized that if I reflected Rita's emotions, she would have the opportunity to feel heard and she would be more open to listening for her own "why" beneath her desire to keep the kids, the house, and all the assets. She got unstuck from the "Joe-cheated-on-me" argument loop. Rita *wanted* everything; the house, the bank accounts, full custody of the kids, but what she *needed* was stability and to be heard. Once I validated her by reflecting how she felt that her whole life was a lie (through active listening, as discussed in the previous chapter) she became less emotionally flooded. Then she was able to articulate what she needed in property settlement: namely, security and a perception of fairness. Things moved on easily from there.

This process seems simple enough. So why is it that most divorce cases last for more than a year, even after the financial disclosures have been made? It's because we get caught in the yes-no paradigm and fail to think about anything beyond what we want, and possibly how the other person doesn't deserve whatever it is they're asking for.

In the earlier chapters, we considered other reasonable explanations for the other side's behavior and learned about formulating the best alternative outcomes and the worst alternate outcomes, both of which are great ways to open your neutral space so you're ready to fully listen. And yet, there's so much more to listening than just perceiving the words expressed, especially as it pertains to our emotional processing of the conflict at hand. In this chapter, you will learn the most magical conflict-busting tip that can help you get unstuck from the most entrenched arguments.

Here it is: Just like Rita did, we spend too much time focused on our positions—the "what"—rather than our interests—the "why." For example, saying that we want to have a date night at a fancy restaurant every week is a position or a "what"; behind which lies our interest or "why": because we need to feel more intimate with our partner, we need to feel special, we need a break from the demands of parenting, a change of scenery, to connect with ourselves, etc.

To get to resolution, we need to unpack the emotion behind whatever it is we are fighting about. This is because our emotions drive pretty much everything. When we're in conflict, our emotional brain kicks our rational brain to the curb.

All too often, our emotions take over and we get rigidly stuck on the "what" of a problem at the expense of "why" we're feeling a certain way about the problem. The "what" of an issue is what we want—usually it is the unexamined knee-jerk demand. On the other hand, the "why" of an issue is the reason or need behind the demand. To get to resolution, needs must be addressed before wants. I was once involved in a case where a mother was trying to deny the father's overnight visitation because of his subpar hairdressing skills. While the daughter's hair may have been important, that issue could have been addressed in a variety of other ways, including teaching the daughter to do her own hair. But the real issue in that case was that the mother was grieving over missing her child during the long stretches of time that she was with her father. Only once we discussed it at length did the mother identify the emotion behind her position, and that is when we were able to move past the conflict and arrive at a parenting plan that satisfied everyone.

You may *want* three million dollars in the bank but *need* to know your kid's college expenses are fully funded. If you were suddenly handed a fully funded college savings account, your need (to feel less anxious about paying for college) would be satisfied and your overall sense of well-being would likely improve. You may still *want* the three million dollars but with your need satisfied, the single-minded urgency to have that three million dollars won't be as all-consuming.

Interestingly, sometimes meeting a need can also satisfy a want. For instance, you may *want* your kids to express appreciation for your efforts made on their behalf but *need* for them to act respectfully. It's likely that if they begin to act respectfully, you will feel satisfied. Once you internalize this important discrepancy, you'll be able to aim for the best outcome in any situation. In negotiation on any issue, understanding this is so vital that I am going to repeat it: You need to understand the *whys* (the needs) before you can address the *whats* (the wants). When you get to the heart of this distinction, you will be able to resolve any issue with greater facility than you could ever imagine.

Even though there are serious consequences to conflating the what and the why, we do that every day. **We talk about, think about, and demand what we want without giving much consideration to why we want it.** When we answer the why question, we unlock the need and that is when we are free to reach consensus. Only by listening to our emotions—and the emotions of others—are we able to break free from our entrenched positions and find common ground between each party's "why." As you develop greater understanding about what motivates you, you are likely to find that many of your conflicts are not necessary. Your relationships will become easier as senseless arguments melt away.

When you know why you want something, you can ask for it more effectively. When your ask is focused on the why, you are likely to elicit less conflict and achieve greater reward and satisfaction. This is because when you're clear on why you want something, you will tend to be approaching the ask from a place of vulnerability. Expressing your emotion or need (fear or desire for calm) is less likely to make the other person feel defensive. You are more likely to find the other person more flexible in helping you to sort options to satisfy your needs. Rather than "fight" mode, you may find they go into "problem solving" mode. Whereas, when you are stuck in a positional debate, the tendency is for both parties to dig their heels into their own positions—and eliminate any opportunity to negotiate reasonably from the get-go. When you understand that the root of endless argument loops is the underlying interest, you will have more efficacious conversations with others and within yourself.

One way to illustrate the "what" versus "why" principle is using the "Orange Allegory." Two chefs were in a timed cook-off with one other chef, and time was running short. These two chefs both needed an orange for their recipes, and there was only one orange available. They decided to compromise, and each took half the orange. As it turned out, one of the chefs needed the juice, and the other needed the rind. In splitting the orange in half, neither had what the recipe asked for. The third contestant who needed a lemon for her entry won the contest, as she had all she needed to prepare the perfect tart. Had the first two chefs held a quick, meaningful conversation about why they needed the orange rather than focusing on what they needed, the outcome may have been different. The Orange Allegory illustrates the importance of asking yourself why you want what you want and to consider the same of others.

This simple shift in thinking is incredibly powerful and you can do it for yourself in your everyday life using the "Why Do I Care?" Inquiry. It's super simple.

The Why Do I Care? Inquiry

This inquiry is my go-to method to quickly decide if the fight is worth it. I use it when I am in conflict at work and at home. It helps me refocus and get to the root of whatever is happening without wasting time spinning in useless argument loops. This inquiry will help you shift your focus to identifying and expressing your "why" effectively. Consider this example:

I once worked with James and Nancy, who felt that their son Kyle's teacher didn't like Kyle and treated him unfairly when it came to discipline in class. James and Nancy's initial position was that they wanted Kyle out of the teacher's class.

But I explained to them that pulling Kyle out would probably not be feasible or the optimal solution. Instead, I had them engage in the "Why Do I Care?" Inquiry. Nancy and James asked themselves why they cared and, quite naturally, got a different and more heartfelt answer: they wanted Kyle to learn, grow, and feel good in school. So, while it may have felt validating for James and Nancy to be united with each other in their dislike of the teacher, they realized that simply acting upon their shared dislike would not help meet their underlying interest—for Kyle to thrive in school.

When we get to the why, we can start to genuinely solve the problem. Rather than becoming insistent on an outcome that may be untenable, by asking ourselves what we care about, we can reach a compromise that includes the specific solutions needed to solve the underlying problem. And rather than believing that the other person is the problem, we can ask the other person to become part of the solution. In the case of James and Nancy, they were able to formulate a list of requests for the teacher, such as asking her to tap Kyle on the shoulder when he called out of turn instead of using public admonishment.

Articulating and owning our emotional interest surrounding the problem rather than assigning blame to others almost always elicits a better response when we're in conflict. We all just want to be heard, and the people responding to us also want to be heard. It's when we shift from being stuck in our position (the "what") to tapping into our feelings (the "why") that we get the emotional support we're truly craving. Owning our emotions has immense power to allow solutions to unfold.

Having someone hear us, even if they only listen neutrally, can offer great emotional relief; it can end the very real suffering someone has when they do not feel seen or heard.[ii] If you are having a hard time figuring out your "why" and the person you are in conflict with is not providing you the satisfaction you are looking for as you work through your process, talking to a therapist, coach, or friend with that express intention can be very useful. As a divorce attorney, I found that even when it was clear that there was no legal basis for a more generous settlement because of a betrayal, very often people just wanted their day in court. They imagined that they would feel heard. But even when they won, the court often failed to provide emotional satisfaction—because its focus is often stuck in the "what" instead of the "why." At court, the judge is doing a math equation, more or less, based on the law and the facts that are legally significant. How you feel or whether your spouse cheated on you ultimately has very little impact on how assets are divided. That's tough medicine to ask someone to accept, but that's the way it is. **That's why often, even when clients get what they want physically, financially, or logistically, they come away unsatisfied emotionally. Our human need to be heard emotionally is what drives so much fighting.**

The "Why Do I Care?" Inquiry can help us identify alternate, and ultimately more satisfying, solutions by figuring out our underlying motivator for the resolutions we're pursuing. But it can also help us go deeper within ourselves to understand what motivates us to respond to situations in ways that are not serving us emotionally, financially, spiritually, physically, or otherwise.

Addressing the "why" is where the magic happens. It's where friendships are built and sensible resolutions unfold. When we listen to ourselves and to others and ask the question, "Why do I care?" we can reap countless emotional benefits.

Discovering Your Why

A great way to begin to uncover why you want the things you want it is to make a list of the things you believe you will miss if you are deprived of what you desire. Looking at that list with your neutral space open will enable you to uncover the mysteries of what drives your desires.

For many years after leaving city life and feeling tied to my young children, I complained about all the things I missed. I missed the adventures of travel and longed for New York City's energy, variety, art, ambition, and anonymity. And I missed my wide network of friends and family. I was unhappy, but I knew I didn't want to upend my entire life again. I knew my bird biologist husband was unlikely to get satisfying work in the middle of the city; plus, I was not sure our family would make the transition in a sustainable way. Living in the city as a family would be way more expensive and complicated than the simple life that I'd built—and yet I wanted it really badly. I felt completely stuck, with no good options for moving forward.

That's when I decided to really engage with myself, and I took my own advice by figuring out what my "why" was. Once I did this, I could then begin to bring in pieces of what I missed into my present existence. You can do the same thing. It's simple and it really works!

Here's how I did it:

First, I made a list of what I missed:

- Travel
- Variety
- Art
- Ambitious energy
- Anonymity
- Family and old friends

Next, I made a list of what I felt like I was missing by not having these things:

- Travel = Worldliness
- Variety = Enrichment
- Art = Beauty, inspiration
- Ambitious energy =
  Motivation
- Anonymity = Freedom
- Family and old friends =
  Connection

I sat back and listened for my why. What I heard was that I felt trapped and limited in my new hometown. I had serious FOMO. But moving back to the city was not the only solution to that underlying problem. With some flexible thinking and creativity, I was able to adjust my present circumstances in ways that I would not have ever thought of had I been stuck in the yes-no fixed thinking. First, I hired a babysitter with an international background who shared her cooking and culture with us, helping to address my need to feel worldly. I made a greater commitment and effort to branch out into the local art community and make more varied connections, satisfying my needs for beauty and inspiration. And I made more of an effort to visit my far-away friends and relatives, deepening my connection with those important people in my life. When the kids got a little older, I wrote the book I'd been dreaming about and created a whole new path to adventure, and a reason to travel back and forth to NYC regularly, allowing me time to regularly enjoy the things I loved about the city.

It's incredible how finding the "why" can create the opportunity for creative solutions. Again, I encourage you to get yourself a journal that you enjoy writing in. It can be satisfying to look back for years to come to track your own progress and the development of your relationships.

When the Other Person Is All about the What

Sometimes, even after we have explored our "why," the person we're in conflict with remains entrenched in their position, or the "what." In this case, we have to use our listening skills from chapter 3 to determine reasonable explanations for their position (their interests or their "why").

To uncover the "why" behind whatever it is the other person really wants, you may need to get behind the ask or the "what." For instance, maybe your employee is advocating that they must have a new title (the *what)*, but in your company, getting this pushed through is a paperwork and a bureaucratic nightmare for what seems like no real change from your vantage point.

If you value this employee, rather than ignoring the request, consider asking some gentle questions around *why* they want the new title. Recalling that the *why* is the need behind the *what or the want*. It is likely you will hear that they need to feel more respect, acknowledgment, or some other intangible. In this case, organizing a lunch in their honor or presenting a plaque to them at an award ceremony may be another way to give them the respect they need in a way that is much more doable for you.

The Why of Hillary and Simone

Looking at the "why" in the case of Hillary and Simone may have brought them greater understanding as well. Simone was angry at Hillary because she thought Hillary was being dishonest. But had she taken the time to consider why Hillary had avoided signing the lease without sharing her concerns, she may have recognized that Hillary was a people pleaser and didn't want to disappoint her. Similarly, Hillary could have realized that Simone was driven by her anxiety around an uncertain financial future for her and her mother. Hillary could have listened for what Simone's goals were, why she wanted a new place, and opened a dialogue about why that worked or didn't work for her. Hillary could have changed her behavior by shelving the conversation about losing the leases, and instead pivoted to how they could support each other with their bigger goals. Instead of Hillary feeling controlled by Simone's take-charge behaviors and Simone feeling irritated by Hillary's avoidance, they both may have felt greater compassion for each other and opened the way for a more thoughtful conversation.

In our more important relationships, such as with a spouse, partner, or close friend, it may be possible to get other people to understand the what-why distinction. But often, it's not realistic that we're going to be able to get other people to understand, or even care about looking at the conflict through this lens. The best we can do is to carefully weigh other reasonable explanations and then tell ourselves a more favorable story to reach greater understanding of why things are happening the way they are. From there we can respond in

ways that satisfy their deepest needs, and therein create opportunities for us to find greater peace.

Thinking Fluidly

It is so important to remember that you don't have to be stuck
thinking about or doing things a particular way. As we grow
older, we often become rigid in how we think. But that doesn't
mean we can't change our minds at any moment. Of course, as
we addressed in chapter 2, making changes in how we view ourselves vis-à-vis the world around us isn't something we can do
overnight. However, by creating new habits of thought, old dogs
truly can learn new tricks. Rigid thinking can interfere with our
ability to make well-reasoned decisions. As we age, we need to
be more mindful of thinking flexibly.[iii] All too often, our rigid
thinking interferes with our ability to make well-reasoned decisions.[iv]

Our mind-set informs our thinking and enables or interferes with our ability to do things differently. Our willingness
and ability to learn about ourselves—our motivations, our
whys, our part in the problem—is determined by our mind-set.
I like to think of myself as open-minded. An example: these
days we hear more about gender fluidity than we ever did
before. My children offered me significant, sometimes painful education that swiftly taught me to begin pushing my own

boundaries around definitions of male and female. I used to operate from a purely binary mind-set based in rigid historic thinking. Over time I have recalibrated my perspectives and realize that the way I understood gender wasn't "right;" rather it was simply ingrained and unexamined. Today I understand that I was looking through a very limited lens.

The act of changing our mind-set and consequently our habits is also learning by doing. Just as learning a new skill is best done by repetition, so too is changing habits and reframing perspectives. The transformation won't happen overnight; it happens moment by moment, each time we choose to act differently than we did before. It may be a conscious decision at first. However, with enough repetition, we can learn to internalize new ideas and behaviors such that they become our default reactions. Our learning isn't a linear process that ends when we achieve our desired behavior; it's a cycle that continues as we move forward with our lives and in our relationships. As we learn more about ourselves, the people around us, and our relationships with them, our ideas, behaviors, and interests might change; and so too our attitudes and mind-set can grow and reflect that growth and change.

Carol Dweck's book, *Mindset: The New Psychology of Success: How We Can Learn to Fulfill Our Potential,*[v] is particularly compelling because of the action word *learn*. In her book, Dweck posits that we think, react, and behave in a particular way unconsciously. We already know that we can change our habits of thinking and behaving, and according to Dweck, we can also change our underlying mindset.

Early in my marriage to Mitch, I chose to transform my single-minded "need" and identity from "I must live in the city" and "I am a city person" to "I am a person who needs variety, anonymity, adventure, connection, and inspiration." With this understanding, I was able to release my attachment to moving to the city and begin to explore more viable options without upending my family and my relationship. Consider ways that you may begin to reframe your perspectives around positions you take in your life or in your relationships that are not working for you. Once you understand your *whys*, you can start to reconsider your *whats*. As you get more in touch with your motivators, you will find a whole new menu of possibility unfolds.

While listening to your inner voice and the messages of those around you is the theme of this section, always keeping your vision clear is equally important.

KEY TAKEAWAYS

- Most conflict happens because we argue positionally (we are stuck in the want, or the "what"). Solutions unfold when we hear the interests behind the positions (finding the need, or the "why").
- Use writing exercises to clarify your beliefs, wants,

needs, and intentions—and understand how situation will change if you don't get the things you want.

- Create a "Why Do I Care?" journal where you can write down the reasons why you want what you want. Consider the following questions: How will your life change? What will it mean to you if you receive the outcome you are seeking? What are the outcomes desired and how does the position support the thing you want most?

- Consider how to develop a flexible (or growth) mind-set versus a fixed mind-set, particularly as it relates to generating new ways of understanding our motivation in conversation and dynamics.

CHAPTER FIVE
You Can Control Your Inner Narrative

Now that you understand the importance of being aware of your own role in conflict and you have started tapping into newfound listening skills, we will now go deeper and take a look at your inner narrative.

When I met Fiona and Sofia, they were both six years old. Fiona loved reading, writing, and making her bed. She had kept a diary since she learned to write at four years old. She was very observant and had a strong sense of self; she said that when she grew up, she wanted to be something "high up, like a doctor." When she visited relatives or her parents' friends, she was expected to give everyone a hug or kiss hello, and as she grew up, she was expected to socialize with the most physically attractive "cool" kids. Her parents admonished her for reading so much and encouraged clothes and toys over books for gifts. She did well in school, but her parents rolled their eyes when she spent countless hours reading.

Sofia, a budding artist, was smiley and whimsical. She was silly, playful, and got along well with other children. They gave her constant messages that she was a unique and interesting; she was encouraged to express her desires and to speak up and not care about pleasing others. On occasions when Fiona and Sofia met each other as six-year-olds, they interacted famously. They played and giggled together for hours until it was time to go home. Watching them play together, I couldn't help but reflect on how the different messages they were receiving at home might impact their long-term sense of who they were and what they would think the world is all about. I wondered how their home environment and the messages they received would impact their inner narratives.

Your inner narrative is like your own personal messaging system.[i] It gives you information about all that you observe, hear, see, and think. It helps you to make decisions,[ii] fast and slow.[iii] These two types of decision-making rely on your inner narrative; quick decisions, in particular, are so dependent on your inner narrative that you do so without even being aware of it. It largely determines how you see yourself and how you interact with the world around you.

You've probably heard the expression "don't believe everything you think." In this chapter, you will uncover that by listening to your inner messaging, you can pinpoint how it is serving you and where the messaging is interfering with your well-being. And you will see that once you notice your inner messaging or narrative, you can start to change your habits as well as the narrative that dictates the course of your life—and improve your relationships.

Understanding your inner narrative is an essential piece in getting along with others, because it informs what you tell yourself about your place in the world around you and how you see yourself in conflict. By listening to the story you are telling yourself with your neutral space open, having a clear understanding of your whys, and engaging your growth mind-set, you can begin to transform your inner narrative into something even better—one that is aligned with your goals and aspirations.

Our inner narratives are shaped over a lifetime. They begin to take hold the second we understand what's going on around us. We unconsciously form our inner narratives for a variety of reasons; sometimes, they explain our circumstances in a value-neutral, unbiased way. Other times, they protect us from powerful negative emotions. Our entire state of being is largely informed by the stories we tell ourselves. However, most of the time, once we understand what they are, with discipline, we can begin to see our circumstances and ourselves in a new light.

According to *Outliers* by Malcolm Gladwell, our environment has tremendous impact on what we achieve later in life.[iv] Further, in *David and Goliath*,[v] Gladwell goes on to challenge how we think about obstacles and disadvantages.[vi] The messages we receive from our parents, and later our peers, have tremendous impact on how we see ourselves with respect to the world around us. Sofia was taught from a young age that she was capable and was encouraged to speak her mind. Fiona was encouraged to downplay her intellectual exploration and expression and to focus on being pretty, "cool," and getting along with others. Gladwell's theory predicts each girl's inner narrative and what that inner narrative will lead them to achieve in later life. Sofia will have cultivated a strong inner locus of control and powerful self-confidence; she would have the confidence to pursue a master-of-the-universe filmmaking path; Fiona would become a highly successful editor but would often feel insecure and would focus on looks and popularity. Our inner narrative can become a deeply embedded loop that informs how we see ourselves, and how we see ourselves impacts how we interact with the world around us.

As we saw with Fiona and Sofia, our inner narratives begin in our earliest years, shaped by our parents, our friends, our family, and our teachers. As such, the way we currently interact with others reinforces our inner narrative, and so our lives ultimately become our inner narrative. While this feedback loop may seem like bad news, the good news is that we have immense capacity to change our inner narrative at any time in our lives.[vii] Even at this very moment.

The Kaboom

My husband Mitch is the youngest of four children. As a kid, Mitch knew his siblings loved him, but nonetheless, he often felt bossed around by them. He didn't like feeling bossed around, and over time he developed a quick reflex to curtail anything that felt like bossiness.

Enter me. After we marry, I tell Mitch a story of a game that my brother and I used to play as kids with another family with a big sister and little brother, just like us. The game was called "Queens and Servants." The other big sister and I were the queens, and the two little brothers were the servants. Suffice it to say that when Mitch feels bossed by me, I am swiftly reminded that he's not the servant and I'm not the queen. My childhood story bucked right up against the part of Mitch's inner narrative that he was not going to be bossed around.[viii] Making matters even more complicated, I had the inner narrative that if I want things done, rather than wait, or complain about how they're done, I better take charge and make them happen. Inner narratives collide and then...*kaboom.*

When we think about our lives, we typically focus on what we do, who we know, where we live, what we own, and other external factors. While we may loosely tie either positive or negative self-worth to these factors, none of them truly define how we feel about ourselves at the most fundamental level. It is our inner narrative that determines how we perceive every conflict in our lives. Mitch's brothers' reasons for telling him what to do may have been perfectly reasonable—he was just a little kid, and they were teenagers. But this experience has shaped part of the man that Mitch became. Because I know about this part of Mitch's experiences, although I am still naturally assertive, I learned quickly to do my best to always include Mitch in decision-making. The thing is, most of the time, we are simply moving through our days, our interactions, and our lives without examining the messages we're feeding ourselves. But our stories impact how we react and respond to others.

Our story about who we are in the world informs how we do everything—what we buy, for whom we vote, how we spend our free time and resources. In today's political climate, often we feel judged; and though we hate to admit it, we are perceived as judging, even if in fact we are only expressing our opinions. Only by understanding how we come across to other people can we begin to build bridges with people with differing points of view. An essential part of this process is to analyze how our inner narrative is expressed to the world around us in conscious and unconscious ways.

Thoughtfully listening to the stories we tell ourselves can give us tremendous power to transcend conflict. Of course, part of the way we behave is embedded in our DNA and could be more than we can counteract.[ix] The nature versus nurture debate is complex and to date is not completely understood. However, as scientists navigate a more robust understanding of how our genes interact, we will one day learn what traits may actually be ingrained in our biology.

For the purpose of this conversation, the assumption here is that most behavior is at least partially learned, and thus changeable through mindful and intentional application of the strategies we have discussed. Most of the time, there is the ability to engage in fine-tuning, at least when transcending conflict, and getting along with others matters. And I would argue that getting along with others *always* matters, as it helps life flow more smoothly, which makes things more pleasant.

Inner Narrative at Work

Let me tell you a little about my friend, Maddie. Maddie and Ella both worked on the same team at a prestigious architecture firm. By all external markers, Maddie and Ella were equally successful at the firm. But from Maddie's perspective, their working relationship was frayed, because she didn't like how Ella "made her feel."

I helped Maddie analyze her relationship with Ella in hopes of improving the situation. The first thing she brought up in our conversation was how Ella strutted around in her Louboutin heels "like she owned the place." It drove Maddie crazy that even though her numbers and outcomes were better than Ella's, Ella seemed to get all the attention from management with her designer attire and Hamptons beach house. Whenever Maddie was around Ella, she found she simultaneously felt "less than" Ella and driven to criticize her for being so "showy." Even though Maddie admitted that Ella was actually warm and funny to her, Maddie never included her in her social plans.

Objectively, Maddie knew that she and Ella had the exact same position and the same salary. Yet, she felt angry and insecure just being around Ella. But I could see that what was happening in their dynamic actually had little to do with Ella. As Maddie began to listen and pay attention to how she may have been contributing to the dynamic between them, she realized that whenever she felt insecure, she became both antagonistic and defensive.

I already knew that Maddie thought of herself as rather financially strained and conservative fashion-wise, even though she was becoming more financially successful each day. I showed Maddie how her inner narrative shaped her low self-worth and strained her interactions with Ella.

Once I helped Maddie become aware of her self-defeating inner narrative, she was able to retrain it. She came to realize that she had the ability to fully restructure her dynamic with Ella. It also dawned on her that she had no idea what was going on in Ella's inner narrative. I then pointed out to her that one reasonable explanation for why Ella was so socially oriented was that she thrived on social interaction instead of specifically trying to curry favor, and that this in no way diminished Maddie and her accomplishments. Another reasonable explanation might be that Ella was trying to compensate for some deeper insecurity of her own. Once Maddie adapted her perception of Ella to incorporate these alternatives, she began to accept projects that were interesting to her even if that meant she would be working closely with Ella.

By owning your inner narrative and reshaping it so it better serves you, you can radically change your day-to-day experience, as Maddie did with Ella. Creating a more positive inner narrative makes it even easier to neutrally consider alternative explanations for the words and behaviors of others—thus creating a greater opportunity to make the "best alternative outcome" a reality.

What's Your Inner Narrative?

Often, we are triggered by other people because our inner narratives inflame one another—like how my husband Mitch's inner narrative about being bossed around and my inner narrative about taking charge went *kaboom*.

This kind of situation comes up all the time. When I was young, I had a fairly new friend who refused to introduce me to her other friends. She lived in a fancier neighborhood, and I felt like maybe she didn't want to introduce me because I wasn't rich enough. Even at the time, I knew it was ridiculous—but that was the story I was telling myself. As it turned out, she had experienced being dumped several times by close friends who hooked up with each other and left her out in the cold.

She didn't want to introduce me to her other friends, but not for the reasons I thought; it was because she was afraid that I might steal them from her. She was making decisions based on her legitimate fear, but I attributed a different intentionality because of my own negative inner narrative.

To begin understanding your inner narrative, it's often helpful to ask yourself questions about how you see yourself as it relates to the world around you. Here are some areas to consider when drilling down what your narrative is. Consider these items on a scale from 1 to 5, with 1 meaning *never* and 5 meaning *always*. Often conflict stems from competing or conflicting ways of seeing oneself.

- I am reasonable.
- I am likable.
- I have good friends.
- I am a good listener.
- I pay attention to details.
- I get my work done.
- I follow up with ideas, people, and commitments.
- When I set my mind to something, I can accomplish anything.
- I am energetic.
- I am strong-minded.
- I am athletic.
- I have passions or strong interests.

- I am creative.
- I am analytical.
- I am stylish.
- I am funny.
- I am dependable.
- I am influential.
- I get things done.
- I am healthy.
- I am punctual.

This list is just a starting point to get you thinking about how you see yourself in the world. And to think about how whomever you are interacting with (or conflicting with) may differ both in how they perceive you and how they perceive themselves. The goal here is simply to begin orienting around what may be going on behind the surface of what we are fighting about.

The Stories You Tell Yourself

To begin unpacking your inner narrative, it's helpful to look at various areas in your life and think about the stories you tell yourself to explain them. This tool can be very helpful both for self-exploration as well as for figuring out why certain relationships are particularly difficult to navigate. In each of the categories below, rate how happy you are in your own relationships, experiences and circumstances on a scale from 1 to

10. Pay attention to any area that you rate 7 or lower, as these are potential triggers for conflict.

Consider your relationship with or feelings about the following basic twenty categories. This list can go on and on, but these are designed to get you thinking about how you feel about your life.

- Yourself
- Your partner or former partner
- Your children and stepchildren
- Your childhood
- Your broader family
- Your coworkers
- Your friends (or your ability to make and sustain friendships)
- Your career/job (and how it impacts you)
- Your sex life and intimacy
- Your environment (inside and outside your home)
- Your money/ economic stability
- Your mental health and well-being
- Your physical health (body image/eating/exercise habits/ sleep quality)
- Your spiritual well-being/emotional safety
- Your time management
- Your physical space/housing/community
- Your level of focus on the past or future

- Your level of flexibility (at home and at work)
- Your personality traits you would like to transform (soften, sharpen, otherwise improve)
- Your education/business

For any of the areas that you rate your feelings at a 7 or lower, ask yourself to consider the root cause of these feelings. Often, we are stuck in feelings originating in history and not in our present day. For instance, you may have plenty of money but think of yourself as poor because of economic hard times in your formative years and so you live in a state of worry that you no longer need. In this case, notice your story, then release it. If you have no idea why you feel a certain way but are able to reframe your perspective without finding out, that's fine. You can just go ahead and dive into the next part of the exercise.

The third and final part of this exercise is to write out exactly what you do not like about the present story or circumstance of each category and then to rewrite it as you would like it to be. What would each area look like if it were a 10? Allow yourself to feel what it feels like to live in this part of your life as though it were just as you wish. Select whichever aspect of your life is most calling you and consider what small action you may be able to make to begin to shift your energy in line with how you wish you felt.

Please note that visualizing perfection won't take away trauma, pain, or poverty. And while it may help you to see the silver linings (where you are rating your life at a relatively high number) it may also be time to seek professional help from a therapist who can help you address the issues at hand. Noticing where you feel satisfied is as important, or even more important as noticing what areas of your life have room for improvement. And in the areas that are suboptimal consider where you have the ability to make small changes. As with habit, small changes made regularly over time can make big changes in our thoughts, decisions and ultimately in our actions. As we change how we think, we alter our experience.

Why all this self-reflection? Typically, the more we feel at ease in our own life circumstances, the better we get along with others. We are less attached to outcomes from any interactions we have with others as our sense of self becomes more at ease and immovable. Interestingly, the more secure we are in our perspectives or points of view, the more flexible we can be in hearing other's perspectives.[x] We are more grounded in how we see things and more able to hear what others have to say without it feeling like a threat.

Reframing Your Inner Narrative

You can dissect and reframe your inner narratives from the ground up to defuse troubled dynamics. Remember, you can always tell yourself a better story—one that is more compassionate and complex. Every so often you may find yourself in an upsetting situation that you just can't seem to shake. When that happens, there's a great listening exercise that can help you access your inner thoughts. I love this one, especially for when you're feeling like you can't quite get a handle on why you're feeling reactive.

First, write down exactly what the situation is and how it made you feel. Ask yourself to find at least ten adjectives to describe your feelings, then describe the story you are telling yourself. Finally, ask yourself to consider other reasonable explanations; as we addressed in the last chapter, consider other ways to look at the situation.

Let's say you're trying to explain to your husband how you think you should manage a financial situation, and he is cutting you off and misunderstanding what you're saying. Write down whatever you're feeling; upset, angry, disconnected, frustrated, disturbed, hopeless, disgruntled, irritated, agitated, and dismissed.

Next, write down your "surface" inner narrative. There's a difference between "surface" inner narrative and the "deeper" inner narrative. The distinction is that the surface narrative is what others see and what we are aware of thinking. Our attitudes (how we think about things or our habits of thought) are fueled by our deeper inner narrative (our worldview, the stories we have been telling ourselves). On the surface, your inner narrative may be that it is impossible to get your husband's attention. This may cause the *kaboom* for you because of something in your childhood. For instance, maybe when you were growing up it you found it difficult to get your mother's attention. Your deeper inner narrative may be that people who you love are often distracted and difficult to reach emotionally.

To engage with other reasonable explanations in this conflict, ask yourself to set your inner narrative aside for a moment and to consider other reasonable explanations. For instance, maybe when he is ignoring you, it is because you caught him at a bad time. Maybe he is on a deadline, and he struggles so much with time management that he is afraid to be knocked off his focus. Maybe when you feel like he is being argumentative, he is just asking clarifying questions in a style that feels confrontational to you. When you remove your narrative, you can start to see that your husband functions on a different time frame and uses a different communication style than you do.

While his way of doing things may sometimes be difficult for you to handle, it does not necessarily mean that he is responding slowly and asking questions with the purpose of trying to antagonize you. Take a breath and recognize that you can ensure the best possible outcome by choosing to be patient, present, and positive. You can then either calmly respond to his questions or ask him whether there might be a better time to have this conversation. By doing this, you can not only avoid conflict with your husband, but also foster a more understanding relationship with him and foster a relationship that is built on understanding and better communication.

Take Control of Your Inner Narrative

The Power of Affirmation: We Are What We Think

If you're feeling stuck and having a hard time figuring out what your present inner narrative is saying, a great way to take control of your thoughts is to neutrally realign your self-perception through a positive affirmation. This can help you both during ordinary times and during times of distress. When we are mindful of our thoughts, often we can powerfully move our lives and relationships in a positive direction. If you believe you or someone you love is dealing with a mental health issue, getting counseling, a diagnosis, and potentially medication is very important, but for issues that don't require that level of engagement, affirmations are a great tool for many to feel better and move forward personally and relationally.

Your affirmation should be:

- Positive
- Specific
- Stated in the present tense

Your inner narrative affirmation can be very simple. Ideally, you will repeat it to yourself throughout your day. Here are some simple affirmations to get you started:

- I am self-confident.
- I am worthy.
- I am strong.
- I am hardworking.
- I am talented.
- I am valuable.

Repeating these affirmations will begin to reset and reframe the way you think about yourself internally and in interactions with the world around you. Please note that if you are struggling with mental health issues, these exercises cannot take the place of work with a mental health counselor and, in some circumstances, medication. Sometimes, mental health issues are persistent and cause more difficult interactions. You may need to consult with a mental health professional to realize that such help is necessary.

Deep Belly Breathing and Box Breathing

Deep belly breathing can be hugely helpful in freeing yourself from anxious thought patterns and cluttered thought. Making space for new ways of thinking can be game-changing when it comes time for reassessing uncomfortable feelings and perhaps conversations. Breathing is a great way to clear your mind so you can press reset and begin to change your inner conversation.

To engage in deep belly breathing, find a quiet space and turn off all artificial light. You may sit either on a chair with feet grounded or cross-legged on the floor. Each round of breathing is done in three steps. The in breath, the hold, and the out breath.

Intentional box or square breathing is another great way to slow your busy mind and clear the noise that is distracting you from the present moment. It takes deep belly breathing one step further by holding the breath at the bottom as well as at the top.

It's similar to deep belly breathing except it incorporates a second holding of the breath at the top of the cycle. In a seated position (preferably with lights dimmed) close your eyes. Just sit and breathe regularly, feeling a nice deep breath where your stomach and chest rise and fall with your breath.

Then, begin your breathing (deep belly or box) as follows:

1. Take a nice long in breath through your nose to a slow count of four or five. Feel your lungs fill with air.
2. Hold it at the top for another count of five (or shorter if more comfortable).
3. Slowly, exhale through pursed lips for a slow count of four or five.
4. Hold at the bottom as you did at the top (this is the additional hold of the breath for box breathing).
5. Repeat five times.
6. Slowly open your eyes.

When you are finished, you will notice that your mind feels a bit clearer and you will be more open to visualizing your ideal inner narrative. But here, to recalibrate our inner narrative, we're going to take it up a notch and incorporate our positive affirmation. With each breath in you are going to silently repeat your positive affirmation ("I am radiantly calm."), and with each breath out, you are going to cast away its opposite (e.g., anxiety). Breathe in calm, breathe out anxiety.

Breathe in confidence; breathe out insecurity. Breathe in security; breathe out instability.

While this practice is unlikely to completely change your inner narrative overnight, with days, weeks, months, and years of repetition, your new story can override the stories that are no longer serving you. Remember: we create stories that shelter us from difficult emotions.[xi] An example: if you were abandoned by a parent, you may decide that parent is a bad person. Taking it further, you may decide that since you are their offspring, you are destined to be the same way—or you may decide to spend your days overcompensating by trying to be all things to all people. Then, as you grow and as time passes, incorporating an affirmation into your breath practice can help you release those harmful narratives and replace them with more constructive narratives. For instance, you can see your disappointing parent as an imperfect human or let go of the anger toward the friend who wronged you and lean into compassion. You can move past hypervigilance and invite acceptance.

Once you realize what stories you are telling yourself, you have the power to change them and make them better. You can change your inner narratives one story at a time. And, in remembering that our inner narratives impact not only us, but all the people living with and around us, we can be motivated to pay closer attention to the stories that we tell ourselves.

Hillary and Simone's Inner Narratives

If Hillary and Simone had understood their inner narratives, imagine how differently things could have gone. Simone had grown up without resources, and it was hugely important to her that she become financially successful at a high level. Had she understood her own inner motivation to achieve and also that Hillary did not have this same need, she may have been able to slow down long enough to have a healthier breakup. Similarly, had Hillary recognized that while she was content with the status quo, Simone was not because of her own backstory, they could have saved their friendship. Had they been able to at least begin to consider their underlying emotional motivations and fears they could have been more vulnerable, less reactive, and more able to reach a place of equanimity and consensus.

Even if they had never discussed their emotions, with self-reflection, their lifelong relationship could potentially have been spared.

KEY TAKEAWAYS

- Recall from earlier chapters that your role in the conflict—and the attitudes, expectations, and stories you bring to the conflict—is just as important as the role of your friend, family member, or colleague. Your inner narrative dictates how you see the world and how you relate with others, so it's important that you take control of it and harness it for the best possible outcome.

- Getting control over your own inner narrative requires tapping into some of the same exercises in neutrality from the section on neutrality in chapter 3 (page 57); try breathing exercises and affirmations to help you take back control and assess your own narratives neutrally during both ordinary times and times of distress.

- Understanding and shifting your narrative is often a creative exercise. To get your creative juices flowing, try out the exercises such as the "What's Your Inner Narrative?" observational exercise that invites you to answer descriptor questions that illuminate characteristics and backstories to bring observed characters to life. Engage in the self-exploration clarity exercise to help you dive deeper into the various stories you're telling yourself around the most important aspects of your life: money, sex, romance, family, friendship, and career.

- By listening to your inner narrative and learning to control it, you can begin to reshape your thoughts and get along better with others.

PART III
Shelving Heated Conversations

This section will teach you how shelving or pausing the most heated conversations (both with yourself and with others) will shift your relationships. Shelving gives time for your emotions to settle and thoughts to marinate so that your outer behavior reflects the changes you have made to your mindset. The self-reflection and listening skills you developed in the first two sections of this book will prepare you to embrace the highly nuanced skills needed to establish firm boundaries, respond instead of react, and dismantle your own natural defensiveness. As with the previous sections, you will learn how to build habits that incorporate each of these skills to create lasting change in interpersonal dynamics across all areas of your life.

CHAPTER SIX
Shelving and Boundaries Will Set You Free

Sometimes less is truly more, or—to take a page from my Grandpa Walter's book—some relationships should just be "shelved" for the time being. He once told me, "Never throw anyone away. Just put them on a shelf." Shelving relationships that are not working in the moment is a terrific way to keep bonds strong during times of strife. Shelving relationships and conversations for a later time can both allow the dust to settle and let unimportant arguments, that may never need to happen, melt away.

For instance, you don't necessarily need to unfriend your college roommate even if her posting supportive images of a politician you hate is driving you crazy. Simply take a break or "put her on a shelf" by pausing access to her posts on social media or limiting how often you see or speak with each other.

Sometimes the best solution is shelving a relationship until the dust settles—but other times, that sort of pause isn't possible.

If that's the case, one great way to start having more positive interactions with people is to draw firmer boundaries around specific aspects of that relationship. Shelving can last for any amount of time. It serves to put a dynamic in a suspended state until emotions have resolved or situations have evolved.

When you feel marginalized by a colleague at a meeting, rather than reacting in the moment, shelve the issue until you've had a good night of sleep or two. It's likely you'll come back more level-headed after a brief reprieve. If your husband challenges you in front of friends, instead of taking him on in public, shelve it until you get home and you're apt to have a more positive outcome.

Sometimes relationships need to be shelved for years. I had a friend I used to talk to every day. Then, in our late twenties, something changed. What used to be a light-hearted, supportive relationship started to feel draining. I found that sometimes after we spoke, I was left feeling judged or misunderstood. It turned out our conversations were also leaving her feeling bad. I had no idea that, for reasons of her own, she was feeling similarly until one day she called me and announced that she still "wanted to be friends" but needed to take a break. I was hurt, but also relieved. Our relationship had turned toxic for a variety of reasons. We remained loosely in touch, and ten years later we started speaking again more regularly. Because of that break, we were able to sustain that relationship for decades. And though we are not in one another's everyday lives, we are there for each other for the most important moments, and she remains one of the people most dear to me in the world.

Sometimes you can't shelve a relationship, but you can set boundaries around the frequency, situations, and subject matter of interactions you need to limit. Boundaries are necessary in every facet of our lives, and there's nothing wrong with setting boundaries when the need arises. For example, when you're younger, you often may feel inclined to go out with office friends several nights a week. But then at a certain point, for any variety of reasons (marriage, babies, politics, yoga class), your needs and desires may change. You still may really enjoy your work friends, but if you find that you feel emotionally drained every time you go out for drinks with your buddies from work, maybe it's time for a change. Consider setting boundaries around how often, which nights, or how late you will stay out, or dialing back on the content you share with them when it comes to your opinions about work politics, your personal relationships, or any other category of conversation that may be better left to share with a different group of friends or to keep to yourself. In all, "shelving" pieces of a dynamic is a great way to continue a relationship without feeling, or acting, fake.

When you still love the people who came into your life because your kids are the same age, your "mom" friends, on a certain level, but the kids get older and no longer have all that much in common, you may find certain relationships less enjoyable than you once did. Rather than proclaim (to yourself or to others) that you're no longer friends by drawing a firm line in the sand, you can simply take a break by gently excusing yourself two out of three times they're still getting together. If you're lucky, life is long, and few things are as rich and rewarding as long-term social connection. Even when you find you have less to say to them than when you were all enraptured and exhausted by your sweet little darlings, there may still be a thread worth keeping.

Sometimes the Best Reply Is No Reply

I have a cousin who once was posting jokes on Facebook that came up in my feed every day. These jokes were mostly political memes that she thought were "a goof" but that I found offensive and rude. I love my cousin very much, and I didn't want to break off our relationship...though I also didn't need to wake up every day to something I found hateful.

So can you guess how I handled this situation? Did I unfriend her? Block her? Did I call her and give her a piece of my mind?

I knew that cutting off our relationship just wasn't the right option. My cousin had shown up for me throughout my life in ways both large and small. When I was a kid, she'd take me out with her boyfriends for movie nights; after I left for college, she would send me gifts. We shared grandparents, Christmases, and hundreds of family dinners. Though her memes came off to me as short-sighted and even hateful, I took stock of the larger situation and acknowledged that my way of thinking may come off self-righteous, condescending, and wrong-headed to her. After going back and forth, I decided to hit the "take a break" option on Facebook. For me, this was the right decision.

But where I missed the mark is by calling her to let her know I'd done so.

In short, our conversation did not go well. What was I thinking? I'd agonized about how to react correctly, only to then needlessly call to cheerfully let her know we were on pause. We lived far away from each other, so it was easy for us to not speak in person for months on end. In retrospect, taking a pause was the right thing to do, but announcing it to her was not.

Thankfully, the next time we saw each other, we had a conversation smoothing over our dynamic, understanding that while we would never align with each other's perspective on the memes, we still loved each other and wanted to be in each other's lives. Had I quietly "muted" her on my feed, she would have been none the wiser, I wouldn't have seen the upsetting memes, and we could have been spared from a fruitless, upsetting conversation.

In hindsight, by prioritizing my whole, rich, and multifaceted relationship with my cousin, I could have put my discomfort about her Facebook posts in perspective. Prioritizing my love for her over our disagreement would have been a better choice from the start. As time passed, our political differences would have likely blown over. There's tremendous power in backing away from a pointless argument loop and much less in escalating it.

As shown in my example with my meme-loving cousin, the

online world has introduced a vast minefield of interpersonal conflict.

Shelving is a dance that can keep everyone's heart singing and feeling connected over the long term. When you shelve, if you are clear and kind, you are likely to have the best results. Here are some starter statements you may consider when you want to shelve a relationship or other commitments but don't want to ghost someone:

1. "I care so much about you and about our relationship, but our present dynamic isn't working for me."
2. "This organization is so important to me and near to my heart, but I'm not sure this position is for me right now."
3. "I so appreciate the invitation, but I am so exhausted I'm going to have to pass this time."
4. "I really appreciate all you have done for me/taught me/ given to me, and I hope one day I will be able to do the same for you."
5. "Next time. Ask me again!"

Now you try:

Write down a situation that makes you feel stuck, trapped, or unhappy. Write the name of the person you will speak with about shelving, and consider how to carefully shelve the dynamic so that the door remains open later. Craft sentences that are appreciative and leave options open for later engagement.

Boundaries Will Set You Free

Sally, a teacher, did her best to be everything to everyone. She bent over backward to please her husband, her children, and her friends. At work, she was the second or third person in the building most mornings, right after the principal and the custodian. She was the head of multiple committees at school, and in her friend group she was always there for everyone. This way of being worked for her for a long time—until Sally noticed she was having a hard time sleeping and was feeling depleted.

In addition, Sally had a lifelong dream of writing a cookbook for kids. She'd set a goal to have the book published by the time she was thirty-five, but life was always getting in her way. She felt she was constantly dropping her book writing "fantasy" in favor of serving others. But most troubling of all was that Sally found she was becoming increasingly irritable with the people she loved most. She'd spent her entire life supporting others emotionally, physically, and financially, and though that approach was no longer serving her, she just didn't have the clarity to realize how exhausted she was. Sally was so enmeshed with so many different people and responsibilities that she failed to even notice that she was not taking care of herself emotionally or physically. She still dressed nicely and looked sharp as ever. Her home was immaculate and her Google calendar was perfectly synched with her Calendly and Zoom, but she still felt like her life was in disarray.

She was starting to become short-tempered with her kids

and her husband. She confided in me that she had recently lost her temper with her husband. She came home from work, found the bed unmade for the umpteenth time, and snapped at him: "I give, and I give, and I give, and you take, and you take, and you take, and I just can't take it anymore." He was perplexed and she was incredulous that he didn't see what he was doing wrong. They didn't speak for several days.

And yet, despite all these warning signs, it took a big argument with a lifelong friend she loved dearly for Sally to realize something was wrong. For the first time, at thirty-eight years old, Sally recognized that something in how she was living her life had to change, or her relationships, her health, and her mental well-being would suffer. Sally needed rest, but she did not know how to give herself space. She had pushed herself so hard that she had nothing left to give. Saying yes all the time had become a bit of a curse. To begin to feel better, Sally needed to start acknowledging her own limitations and desires.

When we begin to identify our emotional limits in relationships, specifically by noting obligations and relationships that drain our energy, we can see even more clearly where we're complicit in the conflict in our lives. A sharper view of that complicity allows us to set clear boundaries—which in turn allows us to accentuate the positive in our lives, have more productive conversations, and enter a more peaceful space even when the obligations and relationships with people we care about may not really be serving us in the present moment.

Clear boundaries are essential for healthy relationships at home, work, and online. Boundaries can be established in several ways. In this chapter, we'll explore the value of saying no; shelving relationships, conversations, or activities that are not serving us; and creating safe haven containers to ensure that our boundaries are being respected. Please note that in cases where we've set a bad precedent by failing to establish strong boundaries, it's often still possible to save the relationship by infusing a boundary into our dynamic at any point in a conflict. It's never too late to shift your dynamic, difficult as it may seem. As we work through this chapter, keep in mind that change is made over time, and we need to continuously check in with ourselves to ensure we aren't reverting to old habits. Even if you are feeling hopeless, as you continue to practice setting and maintaining boundaries, you will notice that you have tremendous agency in changing your relationship to the world around you, even if you are the only one aware that changes are happening. Your new ways of being will elicit a different, more beneficial response from those around you. That said, be patient with yourself, as there will be a growth curve as your own boundary-setting evolution unfolds.

Sally had a few obstacles to overcome. First, she had to realize that she was too accommodating and that she could begin to reclaim balance in her life and in her relationships simply by saying no.[i] Second, she needed to recognize that she had the power to say no, and that her world would not crumble if she started to protect her time and space.[ii] And third, she had to learn *how* to say no, even if it was a bit uncomfortable, without damaging her relationships or feeling excessively guilty.

The Power of Saying No

"No" is one of my favorite words. I know how lucky I am that it's so accessible to me because I see so many people struggle with allowing themselves to even *think* it, never mind say it. Many people, especially women, are raised to believe that we need to be accommodating and that saying no to any request is selfish or even mean. But when we say yes all the time, we do ourselves and our relationships a disservice. If for no other reasons, always saying yes leaves us exhausted and useless. And, at worst, it keeps us too long in inauthentic relationships and damaging situations.

Sally had a habit of saying yes most of the time. She was naturally an agreeable person and was happy to help, but there were times when she wished she could have said no to avoid an engagement that she was too accommodating to refuse. She was in the reflexive habit of being agreeable, and for a long time, this tendency had served her. But now, her accommodating ways were causing both her well-being and her relationships to suffer. She knew something had to change.

Sally didn't need to change her entire personality; she just needed to make a few small tweaks to how she managed her relationship to the world around her. Saying no was the first step.

Rather than doing more than her fair share of keeping the house neat and clean and carting her children around, she could begin to leave it to others (including her husband) to pitch in. Sally liked coming to work early to get her day on track, but arriving early may have opened the door to her being pulled in for unwanted tasks. She said yes to every committee invitation, every social plan, and generally any request made by whomever for whatever. She was so busy pleasing everyone else, she failed to take space to nourish herself emotionally, physically, and spiritually.

Setting aside time for self-care was essential. Sally hadn't had time to exercise, read, write her cookbook, garden, or meditate, and that had left her feeling depleted, raw, and cranky. Her relationships had suffered as a result. After Sally reflected on the ways she was spending her time and energy and reach clarity on the fact that she was part of the problem, she began to listen to what she needed.

By establishing better boundaries, Sally could give herself the opportunity to improve her well-being and relationships with others. By saying no, Sally could create more time for herself to pursue her own desires, which gave her more energy to devote to the people and causes she truly cared about. Sally was able to create space necessary to "fill her cup" so that she didn't end up tired and frustrated with nothing left to give by drawing firmer boundaries around certain aspects of her relationships that may have been contributing to conflict.

Once she identified her why, which was the desire to be

needed by others, she was able to prioritize which people and activities really mattered to her. She drew boundaries around what worked for her and shelved the rest. Sally learned to create stronger boundaries by learning to say no; soon, she began to feel less stretched. By simply backing off from several nonessential committees, Sally had shelved the commitments that were not serving her, and she was able both to be more productive in the areas that mattered to *her*—and to rest.

When Sally was first learning to take space for herself, sometimes the people in her life, who had learned to expect her to assent to their every request, were offended when she told them no. On more than one occasion, her friend Tara commented that she "didn't have to be rude." Then, on Thanksgiving, her sister took her aside and asked her if she was okay and why she was acting so strange lately. With some discussion, Sally figured out that in her attempt to create pockets of "me time," both mentally and physically, she was starting to inadvertently offend people. Sally's goal was not to alienate herself from others; it was to reconnect with herself. She wanted to feel like her life consisted of a series of choices rather than a laundry list of commitments that were thrust upon her. Luckily, with a few tweaks to her style and by embracing the "positive no," which we'll discuss soon, she was able to establish personal limits without cutting people out.

Sally had to learn to set boundaries in a way that acknowledged that she was changing the relationship rules midstream.

The people she had known, worked with, lived with—some of them for most of her life—expected her to be predictably accommodating. Now that she was acting differently—more independent, and even defiant—some people were confused, and others angry. Even she and her husband worked their way through an adjustment period, but over time, they sorted out her newfound ability to self-advocate—simply by saying no.

Having a firm set of boundaries is one of the most powerful ways to create better relationships. Just as we need oxygen to breathe, our relationships often need a little space to flourish—and a little bit of extra air can often allow a troubled relationship to mend. By creating boundaries, we infuse our relationships with breathing space until conflict dissolves.

If Sally's struggle hits home for you, you are not alone.

It's difficult for many people to say no. Like Sally, we may want to be seen as agreeable or as a team player. We may have been raised to believe that if we say no we are going to be viewed as difficult or selfish. We may have received social political and cultural messaging that tells us that is dangerous to say no. We may struggle with FOMO and feel like if we don't participate in an event, we're going to miss out and potentially regret not being there. We may say yes to everything friends ask of us because we truly want to be there for the people we care about. And we may say yes because we see ourselves as "good" or "nice," and not "showing up" may feel "bad."

Of course, saying yes, remaining in an unpleasant

conversation, or just "showing up" even when we don't want to is sometimes necessary. But if we're not careful, our energy can become quickly depleted with overly porous boundaries, and we can become resentful, feel taken advantage of, or feel exploited.[iii] Sometimes to say yes to ourselves, we need to say no to someone else.

It's all well and good to be accommodating, but without knowing your personal limits, there is a risk of feeling depleted, empty, and resentful. For instance, when you volunteer your time to others to the detriment of fulfilling your own responsibilities, you risk missing deadlines and being seen as unreliable. You may find yourself irritated and flooded with the feeling that you are living your life on other people's schedules. You also risk running yourself ragged, feeling harried, and leaving personal goals unfulfilled. When you agree to pay for things you can't afford, you risk not being able to pay your bills (and you also potentially risk your credit)!

Like Sally, always saying yes may cause both you and others in your life to feel anxious, frustrated, and irritated. Counterintuitive as it may be, sometimes rejecting people, plans, and opportunities can improve your relationship with yourself and with others.

The Positive No in Action

Kevin had a history of staying in relationships for too long. He had three long-term relationships before he proposed to his girlfriend at twenty-seven years old because he didn't want to disappoint her. Two years later, just after his wife had begun talking about having children, I helped him through his divorce. As part of our work together, we talked a lot about ways he could say no without hurting someone's feelings.

Learning to say no can be difficult, but it's an essential and lifelong skill.[iv] In many situations, a simple no is all that is required, but sometimes, whether because you are changing an established pattern or you genuinely wish to be asked again in the future, further explanation is appropriate. A positive no is a way to draw a line in the sand without burning bridges, but it can take some practice. When we're not accustomed to setting boundaries, saying no may be difficult. And on the other end of the spectrum, we may also overdo it. This is normal as there's a natural tendency to overdo the boundary setting with an all-or-nothing approach.

Remember Sally from the previous section. As she developed stronger boundaries, she became more comfortable saying no and became more adept at doing it in a smoother, less aggressive way. As we develop a nuanced approach to boundary-setting, our relationships improve. There is tremendous power in a positive no because it paves the path to an authentic yes in the future.[v]

Meanwhile, one of the reasons Kevin stayed too long in relationships is because he could never figure out an exit strategy other than simply ghosting, which felt cold-hearted. So instead, he just stayed until circumstances outside of his control brought his relationships to a natural end. He remained with his high school sweetheart until they left for colleges on opposite sides of the country. In college, he met his second girlfriend...fell in and then out of love. But though he was no longer interested in the relationship, he stayed with his college love until she moved abroad in pursuit of a film career.

When he met his third girlfriend, this time "life" did not intervene and Kevin ended up marrying her simply because he felt like it was the only decent choice he had. It took their divorce to force Kevin to do the work he needed to do to figure out that getting engaged and ghosting weren't the only two options. He could break a relationship off in a kind, clear way by exiting the relationship before it got out of hand.

In the same way, you can consider making a list of kind ways to say no. Find ways that feel authentic to *you*. Kevin learned to say things like, "I really can't be emotionally available the way you deserve right now," and "You are amazing and gorgeous, and I know I am just not the right person for you." Maybe that is not kind at first blush, but ultimately it was authentic and led both him and his disappointed would-be partner open to finding a better match.

A few examples of ways to frame a positive no:

- "I'd love to help you, but it's just not realistic for me to do that now."

- "I'm probably not the best one to help you with this."
- "Yes, that's an idea, and maybe this (name other option) will work."
- "I just can't do that at this moment."

Get creative and create your own! Remember a positive no is firm, clear, and offers a positive alternative, explanation, or promise for the future (but only make the promise if you intend to fulfill it!). Try them on and see how each statement feels by saying them to a friend or partner just as practice. If you make it a habit to practice ways to say no in your daily vernacular, they will be more accessible for you when you're feeling the pressure to say yes when you really don't want to. This is a great way to create healthier relationships and for you to feel better. And remember: no can be a complete sentence.

How Strong Are Your Boundaries?

Are you the kind of person who just can't say no? Do you spend time with people who drain you, or engage in activities you'd rather avoid? If you find that you're always short on time, frustrated, and resentful of those around you and constantly exhausted, chances are you need a boundary tune-up. If you've spent a lifetime occupied by other people's agendas, problems and schedules, establishing your own boundaries at first may leave you feeling guilty. But that guilt will melt away as you start taking better care of your own needs. You may be worried that saying no will stir up more conflict than it fixes, but over the long term, setting clearer boundaries will help you develop more authentic, real relationships within emotionally safe spaces.

Strong Boundaries Exercise

Complete this exercise to evaluate how strong your boundaries are and where you might have room for improvement in setting and communicating them.

Score yourself from 0–5 for each of these twenty-five prompts (0= never, 5= always)

- I do whatever is needed to help others.
- I feel taken advantage of by those I love.
- I put others' needs before my own.
- If I say no, I will disappoint others.
- I place my own needs after others'.
- I often don't speak up for myself and then feel frustrated.
- I find it hard to make decisions.
- If I say no people will see me as selfish.
- Good people are helpful.
- I stay in relationships longer than I should.
- I feel guilty if I say no.
- I feel slightly annoyed at others' lack of respect for me.
- I feel guilty when I take me time. Me time? What's that?

- I often feel like the victim.
- I often feel like other people's needs take too much of my time.
- I worry a lot about what others think of me.
- I automatically believe other people's criticism to be true.
- I say yes when I'd rather not because I don't want to disappoint.
- I resent others for being demanding or inconsiderate.
- I often feel stressed and overwhelmed by others' pain.
- I'm afraid of disappointing others.
- Helping others is my greatest reward.
- I have no time for exercise.

Score yourself between 0–10. The higher your score, the more you could benefit from a boundary reboot. Remember, we are better partners, friends, parents, coworkers, and neighbors when we feel better. Better boundaries give us the much-needed emotional and temporal and space we need to reboot and to be fully present in our lives.

"Fill Your Cup" Boundaries Exercise

If you're not sure whether your boundaries are healthy or you feel that a tune-up may serve you, now is a great time to fill your self-care cup.

First, make a list of all the people you enjoy spending time with and the things you want to spend your time doing. Force yourself to come up with at least ten people and ten things, but make the list as long as you like.

Make a second list of ways you are spending your time. Consider which of these commitments are filling your cup and which are draining it.

Make space in your calendar to spend at least an hour a day doing one of the ten things that make you feel good, and commit to spending time with a person who makes you feel good each day. Make it a priority to keep these appointments with yourself. Eliminating nonessential activities that are causing stress or are not energetically filling you up positively is a great way to create the necessary time.

Then, several times throughout each day, notice how and when your mood or outlook shifts. Write in your journal who you are with, what is happening, and whether your mood shifts for the better or the worse. It is best if you do this over a period of weeks so that you can identify patterns in how you feel under particular conditions. If you notice being around certain friends makes you anxious, consider spending less time with those friends, more time with other friends, or more time on your own. The goal here is to find healthy solutions for you to refuel your battery. Maybe you have a loved one you deeply care about but can manage only in small doses. Consider spending dinner or one overnight together rather than a weeklong vacation. We don't always need to cut off people or stop engaging in activities completely to reap the benefits of setting boundaries—just cutting back the time spent with draining people or on less-preferred activities can make a positive difference.

Review the list of people and activities that fill your cup daily and add to them and delete from them as needed. Make sure that you are giving yourself at least some of what is on this list every day. Continue to notice throughout the day what people and circumstances make you feel positive and negative. Add the positives to your list of people and add to the list of things that fill your cup and limit your negative interactions whenever possible. By saying no and limiting your exposure to things that bring you down, you can create more space to fill with people and conversations that will fuel your positive energy. When your cup is full, you will find it easier to be less reactive, more responsive, and more present in your relationships.

Create Safe Haven Containers

If you're in a relationship that doesn't feel safe, emotionally or otherwise, creating a "safe haven container" can be a lifesaver. A safe haven container is literally a safe space; it can be a physical location that brings your inner energy to a more balanced place, like a therapist's office where you and a partner can have difficult conversations, or a mediator in the workplace or at school where you can work out issues in a controlled environment so things don't spin out of control. It can also be a form of communication that you can check at agreed-upon times. Remember to put your self-care priorities into your calendar with the same level of importance as your other commitments. Consider building in time for safe haven conversations.

In the context of a relationship with a difficult partner or spouse, you may decide to hold off having certain conversations until you're with a therapist. If you're dealing with a difficult, argumentative coworker, consider only having conversations that are planned and when you are well-rested and can be emotionally and physically present. If you're in a friendship that you're attempting to reshape, design your communications in a way that serves your peace of mind. Do not let someone else's impulsive, angry, anxious, or otherwise destabilizing behavior interrupt your peaceful state of mind. Giving yourself a safe space to handle difficult, awkward, or untamed conversations is a great way to manage conflict constructively. A skilled third party may help you to realign your priorities or perspective so that you don't say or do things that you may later regret.

When we feel stressed or emotionally flooded, we may say reactive things. This is especially likely to happen when dealing with someone whose communication style feels more like an open fire hose of information. When I was litigating, I'd often hear clients complaining about receiving emails from their ex while at work. They found the timing of the communication overwhelming and intrusive, making it difficult for them to concentrate on their job. What I found was that by creating a safe haven for these communications by simply setting up an alternate, more controlled means of communication (either on a separate email address or via an app that could be kept off during the workday), the information could be shared without adversely impacting the recipient's day.

Hillary and Simone's Boundaries

If Hillary had stronger boundaries and exercised her ability to say no, things could have gone so differently. By pausing to think about what she really wanted before reflexively saying yes to entering a bigger lease with a larger financial commitment with Simone, a lot of grief could have been avoided. Hillary was so in the habit of pleasing others that she rarely said no, especially to Simone. Then when pushed, she felt taken advantage of and angry at Simone. Simone may have been a bit of a bulldozer by moving quickly, but she was clear in articulating her desires. In this case, in terms of boundary work, the onus was mostly on Hillary. On the other hand, given their long-standing friendship, Simone may have been aware of Hillary's proclivity to say yes when she meant no.

In that case, she could have done some deeper questioning of Hillary before allowing herself to get so emotionally
wrapped up in a commitment that she maybe should have
known was likely not to come to fruition.

KEY TAKEAWAYS

- Explore the continuum between porous and firm boundaries as well as the value of developing the boundary
  muscle so that it supports wellness and promotes better,
  healthier relationships. Learning to say no is essential for
  boundary building.
- Self-care is a key component to boundary setting. Use
  the self-care assessment tool from the exercise to cate-
  gorize where you wish to spend your mental and physical resources versus where you are actually spending
  your energy.
- Explore the concept of shelving relationships, conversations, and interactions and revisiting them at a more
  efficacious time.
- Creating a container around your time and energy can
  likewise create a pathway for your personal success, give
  your relationships breathing room, and pave the way for
  less conflictual interactions.

CHAPTER SEVEN
Defensiveness Is the Enemy of Resolution

When we're in conflict with someone in our life, we're more likely to engage in negative thoughts than when we're feeling good. Our inner narrative determines how we feel all the time, whether we're in conflict or not. Our sense of inner well-being is derived from the thousands of thoughts we have each day, which can be positive, negative, or neutral. After a lifetime of experiences, coupled with our DNA, many of us spend far too much time with negative thinking, which results in us being defensive and impedes us in our quest for a sense of well-being. This negative thinking can impact how we get along with and are perceived by others. And it can keep us stuck in situations in which we feel unrecognized or frustrated.

Angie was stuck at midlevel management, and even though she was talented and hardworking, she felt like she was constantly punching up at work. She sometimes wondered if she was on the brink of losing her job, and she couldn't quite figure out why. She watched herself get passed over by many newer hires for promotions and had been at the same pay grade with the same title for the last several years. Plus, even though there were closer physical location options, and she was fairly senior, she was still at the original worksite, which was further away from her house than she liked to commute. She knew that her reviews at work were less than stellar, but she believed that's because her boss, Sarah just "didn't like her." She felt like Sarah was out to get her for no reason, and that there's no way she could ever get another job.

Her boss felt that although Angie's work product was high level, working with her was difficult. She often arrived late to the office, was very distracted, and typically sent her work in at least a week past deadline. Sarah had her own supervisor to answer to, and Angie's poor time management was making her job increasingly difficult. Angie was singularly focused on her high-quality work product while blaming everyone around her for her own failures to complete tasks on time. Although the quality of her work (when she finally submitted it) was exceptional, her tardiness created problems for Sarah as well as her coworkers, and she refused to take advantage of the help offered to her through human resources. Sarah appreciated Angie's work product and knew that her years of institutional knowledge would take years for someone else to acquire, and yet she felt drained working with Angie and tired of her constant excuses. She also was done with taking the heat for Angie's tardiness on task completion. Angie and Sarah had been going in circles for years. Sarah would call out Angie for being late, and Angie would become defensive.

And then, Angie had an unexpected stroke of luck when the pandemic hit and the physical office closed down. Surprisingly, things began to change for Angie for the better. With the two extra hours to each day gained with the loss of her commute, Angie was no longer struggling with timeliness and Sarah was increasingly pleased with her work. As it turned out, the commute had been too much for Angie, and she had been highly distracted by coworkers all those years when she was working in person. When the office reopened, Sarah reached out to Angie and invited her to continue working from home. Angie was thrilled. Angie learned that working from home had always been an option, but because of their toxic relationship, it was never even raised or considered. In retrospect, Sarah expressed that she wished she'd thought to offer that option years ago; it had simply never crossed her mind.

Angie and Sarah were so caught in their defensive dance that they never had the space or opportunity to troubleshoot and find a solution or resolution. Angie was angry that she was treated so poorly by the company, as evidenced by the location of her office notwithstanding her seniority at work. Sarah was irritated that Angie was sloppy about delivering her work on a timely basis. Neither of them was at all focused on the other's positive traits, or what benefits they got from the other. They each were angry and singularly focused on how disrespected they felt.

When we're in conflict, the heat of our emotions interferes with our reflective abilities.[i] We get stuck in our own story of what's going on; when really, to reach resolution, we must always access our neutral space and try to put ourselves in the other person's shoes. When we do that, we're more likely to arrive at a sensible outcome that supports everyone's needs and point of view. The more we're emotionally flooded, the more likely we are to dig in our heels, repeating the same negative patterns. Sarah and Angie spent years stuck in the very natural tendency to get into the offensive/defensive loop—the "I don't understand how you messed this up" and the "you're a bad boss" loop. Before they could improve their relationship, they had to step back from those emotional reactions and give themselves space to process their feelings in a different way.

Respond, Don't React

To build upon your own self-awareness and improve your ability to be less defensive, it's important to understand the difference between reactivity and responsiveness. Reactivity is the emotional, visceral response to a problem. It's the quickest, most reflexive answer we give when we feel pressured. While sometimes a reflexive answer is also the best reply, often it is the one we wish we could retract. The trouble with reactivity is that it is an impulsive act based on in-the-moment emotion.

When we're reactive, we fail to anticipate the long-term effects on a relationship, and our emotionally charged responses can cause irreparable harm. There is no shortage of ways in which reactivity can harm a relationship. When we're reactive, we're likely to do and say things that will not serve us or our interpersonal dynamics. For example, when we abruptly cut off an unpleasant conversation, we're likely to create more drama and hard feelings. When we shoot off an angry email in the heat of the moment, we're likely to say things that we regret. When we're in the midst of an argument with our parents, partners, or children, we're more likely to say things that we don't mean. A better solution is to take a moment when you're feeling agitated so you can contain your emotions, gather your thoughts, and instead of being reactive, reply responsively.

While reactivity is reflexive and can be impulsive, *responsiveness*, by contrast, is a thought-out action that calmly and carefully considers long-term implications. In this chapter, we're going to work on receiving and responding, but not reacting to even the most intensely triggering people and situations.

Take Your Defensiveness Temperature

Too often, our in-the-moment response is a defensive reaction to feelings of shame. Much like anger, defensiveness comes from our natural tendency to protect ourselves from information we perceive as threatening to our well-being. It helps us to preserve at least our surface self-esteem—and yet it compels us to start pointing fingers and engage in the ever-popular blame game. What is especially insidious about defensiveness is that when we're in the midst of conflict, we often don't even realize when we're acting defensively.[ii] Defensiveness is a learned behavior that can be unlearned, so do not despair. You may be unsure of whether you're defensive. Here is a short checklist for you to take a look at.

Consider if you engage in any of the following behaviors or thought patterns when you feel criticized:

- Try to justify your actions.
- Blame the other person for what they're criticizing you about.
- Stop listening to the other person.
- Accuse the other person of doing the same thing.
- Tell the other person they should not feel the way they feel.
- Feel like you are always under attack.
- Bring up past instances rather than talking about the present situation.

If you find that you are defensive, ask yourself to take a step back and consider what is going on for you emotionally when you're feeling barbed. It's very hard to be vulnerable with ourselves but by getting real with our own shame story we can begin to shift how we respond to those around us.

Blame, Shame, and Defensiveness

Let's take a look at how insidious our natural, instinctive defensiveness can be and explore how all too often it drives a blame-and-shame spiral when we're in conflict. Blame and shame go hand in hand. Rather than forcing us to recognize our potential complicity or culpability in any particular scenario, blame allows us to externalize whatever is happening as happening to us. Blaming others is a form of defensiveness.[iii]

Here's an example of what that could look like. Marla's husband, Frank, is three minutes late to couples counseling. Marla, embarrassed that he hasn't shown up, texts Frank to see where he is, apologizing to the therapist and saying that he must be en route. After three minutes and no reply, Marla then calls Frank three times in a row to see where he is. Frank ignores her first two calls. On the third call, he picks up and is immediately irritated that she interrupted an important work call. Marla is frustrated that she is being blamed for his failure to show up for the session and failure to look at his texts. The therapist asks Marla if Frank will apologize for not showing up and for being reactive. She smiles, stating that things don't go that way in their house. Later on, Frank is irate that Marla called so many times in a row when he had specifically asked her to call no more than once each day. Part of the reason they're in couples counseling in the first place, from Marla's perspective, is because Frank is disengaged, reactive, and "blamey."

Rather than coming to Marla with a calm apology for his behavior and an expression of tenderness toward her, Frank amps up his anger and tells her sternly to *never* do that again. She promises she won't. While it may seem like Frank is getting what he wants in the moment, he has pushed Marla away emotionally, which ultimately does nobody any good. Defensiveness thwarts progress.

People who feel shame tend to internalize and personalize everything that happens to them. Shame typically results in either attacking the self or attacking others.[iv] Frank isn't a bad guy. He's just got a shame story a mile long and has the need to blame others to keep his own ego intact.[v] When we feel shame (internalized bad feelings), we feel pain and will do anything to stop the pain. Frank felt bad about missing the meeting. He also felt bad about himself for getting so easily derailed by his wife calling him during the day. He had internalized shame for his deep tendency to be easily derailed or distracted when he's concentrating on something. Rather than addressing his painful shame story, he protected his own ego and directed his emotions outward toward Marla. Blaming someone else for one's own shortcoming or an undesirable result or outcome can serve as a short-term release.[vi] The problem is that blaming others for our action or inaction is only going to increase tension and keep us from having deep relationships or even positive interactions with others thereby causing us even more shame over the long term.

Disrupting the Shame–Blame Cycle

All hope is not lost, however, as there are some simple ways to begin to break your shame–blame cycle. The first step is to take the time to recognize when it's happening. As we learned back in chapter 1, we are often more complicit in creating our own problems than we initially realize. The good news is that if you had the power to create a problem in the past, you likewise have the power to prevent the problem in the future. The next time you find yourself being defensive, take a moment to ask yourself if you are feeling attacked. Notice whom you feel attacked by and consider the perceived attacker's *why*.

Agatha and her parents used to have huge blow-ups around her ideas about marriage and family. She and her boyfriend were living together with no obvious plan to marry, and her very traditional parents were disappointed and worried about her future. For a long time they went in circles, with Agatha trying to justify her choices and explain her reasoning to her parents. It never went anywhere, and over time this argument eroded the quality of their relationship.

Agatha was so depressed that she began to feel alienated from her parents, whom she loved very much. But then, by temporarily shelving the conversation, and taking a few deep, calming breaths, she recognized that she was asking her parents to accept something that to them felt shameful (shame was their why). And, at the same time, she was feeling internalized shame for letting them both down. And so, round and round they went until Agatha decided to just back off. After taking a moment to calm down and consider her parents' opinion, she did not capitulate and marry her boyfriend, but she did allow her parents the space to air their worries without giving in to her own shame/blame/defense cycle. Agatha was able to defuse the conflict by taking a step back so that she could respond rather than react defensively. Her parents didn't stop worrying about her, but Agatha was able to avoid internalizing their concerns, and their interactions gradually became less fraught.

Whether or not you realize that shame is at play, when you find yourself in a defensive cycle, ask yourself if the argument is worth harming the relationship. Maybe it's time to draw firmer lines around this particular interaction, but "going to the mat" may not always be worth the price.

Shelve for Responsiveness

One way to foster responsiveness, rather than reactivity, is to step back and shelve as a way of setting a boundary with great intentionality—briefly shelving a conversation so that you can take a mindful break in the heat of the moment to gather your senses can make all the difference in your response. Before lashing out, use shelving to take the short burst of space that you may need to be more responsive, less reactive and less defensive. As simple as it sounds, it is a game-changing skill that will help you to observe your thoughts and practice the listening skills from the first two sections of this book. It can be used to slow down a situation that is otherwise a hotbed for conflict. This process is about taking a quick break as a better way to self-regulate and handle an issue as it comes up in the moment.

Here's an example of conversation shelving in action: Arielle and Ken are the parents of two school-aged boys. After thirteen years of marriage, they came to me to mediate a trial separation during the COVID-19 pandemic quarantine. Arielle felt that Ken was overbearing and impossible to deal with. Ken felt like Arielle was controlling and reactive. Normally, I would have worked with the parties on figuring out a housing strategy, a parenting plan, and financial arrangements and done my best to keep them out of court. But, because of the pandemic, Arielle and Ken were not in a position where either person could move out of their home. We had to strategize creatively so that they could live in peace during this period of limbo.

With Ken and Arielle, things went from zero to hot mess in a flash. By shelving, they were able to put certain conversations on pause so they'd each have time to cool down, take a step back, and consider whether whatever they intended to do or say was going to be productive. We established new household communication rules that they both agreed to respect. The rules were quite simple and involved shelving or taking a pause. The first agreement was that since Arielle felt overwhelmed by Ken, rather than react, she would simply shelve the conversation by asking for a ten-minute time-out. Then, at the end of the ten minutes she would either respond to Ken calmly or request an additional ten-minute time-out. The second agreement was that Ken would back off after Arielle asked for space. And finally, they agreed to shelve any issue they could not productively address and established a time once a week with a therapist—the designated safe haven space—who was there for them to troubleshoot when taking the pause or time-out simply was not enough.

For six months, both of them abided by the strategies we developed together. In their case, they both were invested in finding ways to make the interaction smoother, so it worked really well. But what if you don't have two-party buy-in? That's still okay. You may be surprised to learn how much you can change an interaction just by adjusting your side of the equation. If Ken simply backed off or if Arielle slipped out for a quick walk around the block, they could expect similar behavioral shifts.

Sometimes all we need is a few deep breaths to calmly respond to conflict, but other times simply creating temporal or physical space between the person or situation in question is a great first step.[vii]

This pause allows us emotional freedom even while processing difficult dynamics. When you take a "time-out" for yourself, you are essentially giving your body and mind the opportunity to cool down.[viii] During that reprieve, you can decide whether a particular conversation needs to happen, or how deeply you need to engage in the discord. It may be that during the time you gave yourself to reset, you realize that the issue in question is not something that matters to you. Releasing attachment to conversations or even outcomes can make all the difference in your day-to-day well-being.

Making a Pause Work for You

To briefly shelve a conversation, you might excuse yourself in a respectful way. For example, let's say you're at work and engaged in a heated argument over text with your child, parent, or dear friend. Rather than lashing out at them or ignoring them, consider writing them a note stating, "I hear what you are saying and even though we disagree, I love you. But I need a [two-hour] break from this conversation." And then, if the circumstances warrant it, block the caller for [two hours] so you can get through your day. Before re-engaging with the person, check in with yourself so that you are ready to gracefully exit yet again if necessary.

Think back on some of the examples we've looked at so far. Agatha was able to calm herself and avoid becoming defensive just by taking a few deep breaths. Arielle and Ken were able to have a much smoother and more productive separation process when they each learned to shelve for short periods of time. With fifteen minutes alone or a walk around the block during the heat of the fight, they were able to come back and talk things through at a much higher level.

Similarly, as Sally was learning, there was an alternative to issuing a knee-jerk yes or no response, she began to take a pause so that she could respond to requests after thinking them through more carefully. Shelving could have done wonders for Hillary and Simone, who, instead of creating the space they needed to prevent reactivity, simply blamed, shamed, and ran.

By allowing ourselves to pause, we settle our emotional selves and reengage our thinking brains. With a calmer mind, we can make better decisions and avoid unnecessary conflict.[ix] There are timeless benefits from going to a neutral or separate space (mentally or physically) and taking a "time-out" in order to dial down our reactivity and mindfully respond to conflict. Taking some "you" time—and breathing—can do wonders. In only a few minutes, you shift from being reactive to being responsive. And with measured responsiveness, you will achieve the best outcomes, no matter how the conflict-charged situation is.

Shelving is an easy in-the-moment tool that can be utilized to keep yourself from saying things that can't be unsaid and doing things that can't be undone. With that pause, we are better able to listen to other people's perspective or story. The pause is what gives the ability to shift away from defensiveness toward viewing things from a place of equanimity. It enables us to clarify when we're becoming defensive (or someone tells us that we are) so we can interrupt that negative pattern. And once we use our pause to tell ourselves the story of what is happening from the other person's perspective, we're better able to notice when we're becoming defensive. Then we will have the wherewithal to optimize our behaviors and turn a relationship dynamic from contentious to calm.

Shame-Busting Affirmations

Even after shelving a conversation or relationship, addressing the feelings of shame that may arise during or after a conflict can be difficult. It requires you to acknowledge your own humanness, including your own flaws and shortcomings. We feel shame when our shortcomings are exposed to others or even to ourselves. We feel bad and judged; shame causes us to feel a slew of uncomfortable emotions: unappreciated, rejected, used, useless, powerless, and disrespected. In order to push away these uncomfortable emotions, we often externalize our feelings and attack or blame others. Feeling shame is a normal part of being human, but we don't have to resort to defensiveness and blame. By acknowledging and accepting our shortcomings we can take the first step to avoid falling into the blame–shame cycle.

Recognizing our own imperfections can be scary, but it can also bring great reward. We can both feel better living more authentically—warts and all—and we can have more honest, compassionate, loving interactions with those around us. A great way to begin to counteract feelings of shame is by incorporating a positive affirmation as discussed in chapters 2 (page 37) and 5 (page 124) with meditation into your day.

Most of us have strong emotional armor protecting us from shining the light of shame back on ourselves. In my divorce practice, I am accustomed to working with people who are flooded with shame and consumed with feelings of being "less than." Although it is, strictly speaking, not legal work, I often encourage my clients to begin to accentuate the positive in their life by bringing a positive shame-busting affirmation into their vernacular. The thing is, when you start to send yourself more positive messages regularly, you are primed to think more clearly. The same holds true for all of us in our ordinary lives, regardless of our relationship status.

For example, imagine your partner highlights something they perceive as "wrong with you"—maybe you're always cold, you're too loud, or you're somehow imperfect. When this happens, the natural reaction is to go on the defense and counteract with what's wrong with *them* or even blame them for causing your behavior. It's likely that they just poked one of your personal shame stories. You may simultaneously feel annoyed that they don't love all of you and at the same time, you question if whatever they are saying is a real problem with your personality. And maybe you fear you aren't worthy of their acceptance.

In response, imagine you attack and call your partner too sensitive or self-conscious to rehabilitate your sense of self. This shame/blame/defensiveness cycle does not serve you or your relationships. Instead, you can create a positive affirmation to begin recalibrating how you feel by changing the stories you tell yourself. In this example, a great affirmation may be "I am deserving of love and acceptance." When you truly believe that, you will feel slightly less triggered when your partner voices their irritation with you, and you're more likely to have the wherewithal to take a step back. After shelving and considering why what they said is hurtful or not productive, you may choose to calmly engage from a place of calm reflective thoughtfulness rather than emotional reactivity.

It serves us to get in the habit of incorporating a deep belly breathing round of five or ten breaths as described in chapter 5 (page 125), together with a positive affirmation to keep our mental state. That way, even when we're triggered by something, we're more likely to access our neutral or even positive point of view. While it may be impossible to completely change how we see the world, we do have the power to at least change a little bit about how we see ourselves. We have the power to plant seeds of new, more positive thoughts which can serve to counteract even the deepest wells of shame.

The Power of Meditation

Emotional flooding fuels the shame–blame cycle, which creates defensiveness and breaks down our communication.

It goes something like this:

1. We feel bad (shame).
2. We deflect (blame) in our minds.

3. We act defensive.
4. No consensus or understanding is reached.
5. We feel worse.

When we feel upset, it's often because we're focusing on an unfavorable past event or we're worrying about an unwanted set of circumstances unfolding in the future. Tapping into our present-moment awareness empowers us to simply notice all that is, without a care for what should have been in the past or might be in the future. Meditation is a simple practice that allows us to go inward and slow down whatever emotional swirl we may be experiencing in any moment. It helps us to access *present-moment* awareness. Slowing down the flow of unwanted negative thoughts or feelings enables us to reflect, consider alternate possible outcomes, and adopt a less defensive communication style. Present-moment awareness can allow us to take the much-needed space we need to open us up and to figure out why we want what we want rather than going into the all-too-easy and familiar attack mode.

As we discussed with deep belly and box breathing, consider incorporating a shame-busting affirmation into the box breathing practice to increase your feelings of well-being. Each time you breath in, simply use the five count to repeat the affirmation to yourself. Allow this intentional statement to flow through your mind. This is a great way to begin making positive headway in developing the skills to slow yourself down next time you feel triggered. Recall that intentional breathing brings a feeling of calm both to your mind and body. Doing this daily when things are calm will make it feel more natural to do when you're feeling reactive. Even if you are not someone who enjoys this kind of thing typically, you may find after a few days that even if it feels a little strange at first, the hidden benefits are worth the weirdness.

As discussed earlier in chapter 5, your affirmation to be impactful it must be: *positive, specific, and present* (as if it's happening now). Personally, I tend toward anxious and reactive. To counteract this tendency, I have adopted a personal shame-busting affirmation, which is "I am powerful." I remind myself of this often throughout the day. It's my meditation and repeating it often makes it more accessible during the most stressful times.

Here are some personal shame-busting affirmations to try on throughout your day. Remember, if you make it a habit to repeat your affirmation to yourself when you're feeling good, it will be more accessible to you during heated times.

- I have agency.
- I am powerful.
- I am deserving.
- I can do hard things.
- I am perfect just as I am.
- I am confident.

- I am worthy of trust.
- I am smart.
- I am loving.

The goal is to develop a new story to tell yourself so that you counteract your feelings of shame and insecurity. Create a positive affirmation to counteract whatever negative story you are telling yourself. For instance, if you feel insecure, tell yourself, "I am confident." If you feel "anxious" repeat the affirmation "I am calm." When we feel better about ourselves, we're less likely to feel shame and to act defensive and blame others.

Moving from Contentious to Calm

I have a friend, Cassandra, who works as a school principal, even though she was hired much more recently than many of the teachers at her school. She noticed these more senior teachers growing defensive whenever she asked them to perform certain tasks, or when she proposed changing certain schoolwide protocols. At first, the teachers' pushback was tough for her to swallow, and she felt herself feeling defensive of her agenda. But she combated this impulse and gave herself space to settle. She came to me to vent. She felt irritated and defensive about how the teachers were treating her, but she also wanted support to think of ways to troubleshoot these issues.

I asked Cassandra to think about the teachers' perspectives. She thought about what it must be like to have taught for thirty years and then have a supervisor who is decades younger than you trying to change the way you've been doing things for your entire career. Once Cassandra was able to see matters from their position, she adjusted her thinking and started making changes to how she engaged with her staff. The time she took to reflect on their perspective gave her the powerful opportunity to build compassion and work toward putting conflict to rest. She made adjustments in how she rolled out the schoolwide changes so that her approach was gentler and better received. Shelving allowed Cassandra time and space to consider other stories that may have been fueling the teachers, allowing her to open strong channels of empathy.

This same skill applies in our interactions with friends who are on different sides of the political or social spectrum, and with our parents and children. Once we have set boundaries and have temporarily shelved difficult conversations, we are ready to face the challenge of truly seeing things from the other person's perspective. Now that you understand how to say no and when to shelve conversations or entire relationships, you can begin to notice whether you're feeling shame, being defensive, or blaming others. With these strategies, you can confidently bring your internal changes in alignment with your external behavior.

Hillary and Simone's Default to Defensiveness

Hillary could have benefited from understanding that defensiveness is the enemy of resolution. Rather than taking things slowly and going through the YES Method, Hillary and Simone did what many of us do when confronted with a difficult situation: they each became defensive and fed into a negative spiral, which ultimately caused the demise of their relationship.

Instead of recognizing the dangers of defensiveness, forcing themselves to shelve conversations momentarily, and look at the situation from a place of centered neutrality, they became defensive and "blamey."

But it didn't have to go that way. Rather than rush to blame, they could have paused before lashing out and saying things that could not be unheard. During a brief time-out they each could have considered a more metered and productive way to handle her big feelings without finger-pointing. If Hillary had shelved, she may have realized that her lack of ambition was actually not a deficit, rather it came from a place of contentedness. She could have shown greater compassion (rather than judgment and defensiveness) toward Simone. Similarly, if Simone understood what her motivators were and why Hillary did not share them, she could have had the patience to respond more slowly and refrained from saying hurtful things in the heat of the moment.

KEY TAKEAWAYS

- Defensiveness is the enemy of resolution. When we are defensive, our heels are dug in and we can't put ourselves in the other party's shoes.
- You can cope with defensiveness gracefully by exploring your core values, building your self-confidence, and developing a growth mindset.
- Shelving creates a powerful opportunity to build compassion and work toward putting conflict to rest.
- Through the exercises in this chapter, you can be inspired to find creative ways to optimize interactions. Embracing a pause, meditating, and reciting affirmation are just some of the tools you can use to de-escalate high-conflict situations and recenter yourself in order to be responsive rather than reactive.

PART IV

Yes, You Can Get Along

Even after you've done the hard work of the YES Method, (you've owned *your* role, understood the *emotional* story, and *shelved* heated conversations), you may still be facing significant disagreement and discord. This section is all about breaking through longer-standing, deeply entrenched conflict—in part by building upon the work from the first three sections—to strategize, reflect, and ultimately leverage the power of vulnerability and visualization. This section will ask you to consider whether the YES Method is working—and if not, to consider why—and how you can explore your thoughts and feelings even more deeply as you strive for self-improvement and more fulfilling relationships.

Part IV is where the rubber meets the road in reaping the benefits of the YES Method. If we are living too much in our heads and not leaning into our emotional heart space, it's nearly impossible to cleanse unnecessary conflict from our lives. This section will ask you to notice where you are feeling stuck in conflict and assess your vulnerabilities. Moreover, this process will introduce the VIR Protocol™, a getting-along secret weapon that asks you to use the power of visualization to recalibrate even your most difficult relationships. Finally, you will learn how to avoid senseless argument loops without cutting off communication. Having already built strong habits and thought patterns and engaged in the effort of optimizing your relationships with friends, family, coworkers—and the process of conflict itself—you will exit this section feeling prepared to handle even the most difficult of interpersonal clashes and to achieve true emotional freedom from conflict.

CHAPTER EIGHT
The VIR Protocol: Your Secret Weapon

Even if you've followed all the instructions in the first three sections, it's possible that you will still feel stuck in particularly challenging patterns and dynamics. After all, conflict is not always an easy, straightforward topic. And conflict resolution is not a zero-sum game. We may believe there are "winners" and "losers," but, if we want to move forward with a better dynamic, the road to resolution can often become entrenched in a story that's a bit more elusive. An all-or-nothing mentality is easy to latch onto; however, it rarely creates a truly whole-hearted sense of peace. Some people are more concerned with being right or winning than creating harmony. But while being right may be satisfying the short term, in the long term, it will not do much for you or your relationships. If the idea of having truly healthy relationships, even with those people you find to be challenging, is compelling, the power is in your hands. It may be time to take a deeper look within yourself and get to

the core of what's getting in your way to making the relationship better.

Of course, I am in no way suggesting that you can cure
someone else's impossibly difficult nature, untreated mental
health issue, or disagreeable perspective. There are situations
where walking away from a dynamic makes the most sense.
It's always a balance of the relative importance of the relationship, the importance of the issue of the moment, and the
ability and willingness for both parties to engage respectfully.
Sometimes words are best left unsaid. But even when you
cannot make your communication and relationship perfect,
most of the time there are ways to make it better. And *better* is
a great place to be.

Getting vulnerable with yourself takes hard personal and
interpersonal work. In this chapter, you will mine your own
thoughts and feelings in pursuit of growth and strategizing a
healthier solution for embracing the conflict in your life. By
acknowledging your own insecurities or emotionally vol-
atile hotspots to yourself, and by visualizing the future of a
dynamic as you wish it to be, you will gain greater insight into
why you're stuck somewhere within one of the steps of the
YES Method. You will begin to transcend being intermina-
bly trapped in an unpleasant dynamic. Being vulnerable is all
about getting clear on *your present feelings*. Owning how you
truly feel, as uncomfortable as it may be, will serve as your
launchpad forward. When you are in conflict, check in with

yourself and see what comes up for you. Do not get stuck in a negative or obsessive loop; rather, notice how you feel. From there, you can start activating your inner agency to move toward something better.

Think of these final chapters as upper-level skill building to reinforce the lessons earlier in the book. Once you get real and notice your vulnerabilities, as the esteemed Brené Brown, author of *Daring Greatly*, has taught us, you will have more power in your life. Naming them and utilizing your self-worth affirmations to combat them will begin to help you release them. In this section, we are going to give illustrations and more concrete guidance that will help you transcend your present perceived limitations. Once you are more vulnerable with yourself, then you can truly access the YES method.

The VIR Protocol

The VIR Protocol is a framework I developed over many years to help my clients start interacting and living more intentionally, especially with people who drive them crazy. The VIR Protocol is especially useful when you're stuck in a senseless argument loop, and you are living in blame, shame, or anger, but you can use it in virtually every aspect of your life. The goal of this process is to move from blame into the realm of agency. Using the VIR Protocol, you can begin to see your difficult relationships through the lens of best possible conflict outcomes. It acts as a kind of power booster to the YES Method and helps you integrate each step more fully into your life.

The VIR Protocol involves three steps:

1. *Visualize* what you want (your highest goal for yourself or in your relationship).
2. *Internalize* whatever that is (as a daily practice by writing, or by doing some specific action that brings the visualization into your being).
3. *Realize*. Realization is a state of noticing, and is the culmination of *visualize* and *internalize*. The realization is what happens when you have fully internalized your visualization. You embody what you dream. There is no doing, only allowing and accepting.

To bring in the VIR Protocol, visualize the narrative you wish to have. Using mindful affirmation, you can begin to recalibrate your inner story by overwriting it with something better. Our thoughts are like little seeds that we are planting in our mind, so be very careful with the words you use. It's best if we choose the messages we want to send ourselves carefully.

Here's how the VIR Protocol works in practice:

Imagine you're experiencing conflict at work. Last year, you were passed up for a promotion for the second time. You're hoping to finally get recognized this year for all the great work you have been doing on a major initiative for your company, but you have a sense of impending doom. While you may feel defensive about it on the outside, internally you may feel invisible or disrespected at work. You are starting to feel like you should just give up.

Step One: Visualize

Visualize: First, write down goals for your relationships at work. Make a list of what you wish to feel at work, about work, and about your coworkers. Start with the larger picture, and then get more granular. As you dig into the details of how you wish to feel and what you hope to create, you will begin to feel a shift in your state of being. Even if it's uncomfortable to admit, if you want more respect, begin to visualize others coming to ask your opinions or advice about how to handle certain work responsibilities. Remember, your goal must be related to you and things in your direct control—not related to someone *else* doing something.

You may not be able to get a coworker to stop talking about politics, but you can go out of your way to swiftly exit conversations. You may not be able to will your boss into giving you a raise, but you can ask for more money and you can look for other companies that may offer higher pay. You may not be able to stop your spouse from being reactive, but you can respond differently to their behavior. Visualize yourself being part of important conversations.

Decide what your dream or vision is for any aspect of your life. Focus on having a sense of internal balance and outer ease in a particular relationship. Visualize your goal until you can literally see it, feel it, and smell it. Your vision sets the tone for your relationships and for your life.

Step Two: Internalize

Internalize: Here is where your vision seeps into all facets of your being. If in step one, you are envisioning yourself being respected at work; in step two, you are considering what that feels like. You may have felt invisible, and now you have inner conflict about what it means to be truly confident. It may even make you uncomfortable to see yourself in that position, but that's okay. This is your journey and your process. You are carefully considering which elements comprise confidence, and you're trying them on for size. Maybe you decide that a confident person is a leader, so one way to internalize this is by taking on a leadership role in your office or joining a commit-tee related to your profession. Maybe you decide to dress in a more professional way. Maybe you decide to become a mentor for others. During the internalization phase, you gradually embody your vision. You imagine it in a detailed way. Once again, you must be truly vulnerable with yourself to internalize your vision and invite a sense of self-compassion. This self-compassion will serve to help you to dispel any conflict, inner or outer, that you may have around the positive meaning of confidence. It may be that during the *internalize* process that you decide to pivot your visualization for any variety of reasons. Keep going deeper to fine-tune your goals to meet your ever-evolving vision. Here is where you become almost obsessive about the goal. To internalize, you need to become open to receiving whatever it is you are seeking. You need to believe that you deserve whatever you are visualizing. The internalization process is where your intentions are solidified.

Keep your mind focused on your vision.

Step Three: Realize

Through your mindful visualizing and internalizing, you can realize your goals. You can truly reshape your relationship with those in your purview by making shifts in what you see and how you relate. Realization is where your visualization fully comes to life, thanks to all the work you did in the internalization phase when you started to bring your clearly articulated vision to life. As you start dressing for success, getting more involved in your professional organization, or training mentees, you are likely to find yourself actually becoming more confident.

Just like the YES Method, the VIR Protocol requires constant evolution. As we internalize our vision, we learn and grow. Through our own evolution, what we want may change.

As your goals change, come back to the VIR Protocol to visualize, internalize, and realize these new goals. Remember, your thoughts influence your behavior, which, in turn influences outcomes.

It is crucial to be able to name any emotion that is getting in your way. When we accept our vulnerabilities, own them, and release our strong emotions—such as by combating them with our self-worth affirmations—we gain the power to implement the transformational strategies that allow us to realize the outcomes we initially visualized for ourselves. We can move our relationships forward, introducing new dynamics by transforming ourselves and our approach to the relationship. This transformation happens without us consciously *doing* anything further; realization is a consequence of the shift in our consciousness and behaviors.

The VIR Protocol in Action

Joni is a woman in her early fifties. She has one twenty-four-year-old daughter, Olivia, who recently graduated from college and is living across the country with her boyfriend. Joni's been divorced three years. Six months ago she started dating Eddie, a man fifteen years her junior. Olivia knew all about Eddie right from the start. She and her mother have always been close but because of the physical distance between them, Olivia assumed this relationship was a fling and was blown away when she heard that Eddie was moving in with her mother. After hanging up, she texted Joni not to call her and that she would reach out when she was ready to speak.

At first, Joni accepted this, figuring that Olivia would come around. But after week three of radio silence, she began feeling desperate. Joni was devastated. She knew that Eddie and Olivia were close in age and she anticipated some reaction from her daughter, but not to this extent. Joni had been cheated on by her ex and she was disappointed that Olivia wasn't happy for her.

Meanwhile, Olivia was too upset to call Joni and didn't know what to say to her. Was a partner with a fifteen year age-gap really necessary? Eddie was practically the same age as Olivia's own boyfriend. But despite her present anger and feelings of betrayal, she loved her mother, and wished to remain close to her. At the moment, she put Joni's Facebook feed on mute and confided to me that right now, she just couldn't bear see images of mother in this new relationship without feeling like she was going to blow up at her.

After Olivia and I talked about her feelings, she masterfully navigated her way through the conflict. Rather than blaming and dismissing Joni, she tapped into her own power by getting vulnerable. She recognized how powerless she felt over her mother's relationship and released her anger. She allowed herself to feel the hurt running through her. She cried and cried until she experienced an internal release. Her vulnerability is what enabled her to walk through the VIR Protocol. She first visualized what she truly wanted. She exited her mind's blame-and-shame loop by visualizing how she wanted to feel: at peace, or at least accepting of the circumstances. As she allowed herself to feel her feelings, rather than externalizing them or pushing them away, she felt a tremendous release. Olivia began to forgive herself for holding onto anger and disappointment.

Next, she visualized her relationship with Joni as close and loving. Just thinking about it any other way brought tears to Olivia's eyes. She allowed them to flow and to pass. Then, Olivia internalized the belief that it was okay for Joni to have a relationship that doesn't make sense or was even mildly offensive to her. By internalizing what "close and loving" felt like, Olivia was able to tap into a deep well of positive emotional memories with Joni. The more time and intention she spent visualizing, the more she internalized a recalibrated relationship with her mother. The fear of lost connection with her mother began to dissolve. She was able to engage with Joni once again without judgment and anger by focusing on her positive emotional memories rather than their present disagreement. She internalized the sense of peace she'd been longing to bring back. She knew she may never see understand Joni's relationship with Eddie, but still felt more grounded.

Olivia was then able to reintegrate Joni into her life as she has fully visualized and internalized, thereby realizing the peace she wanted to feel in their relationship.

Visualizing and internalizing are an iterative process. As

you internalize your goal, your visualization may become more clear, or it may move slightly in a different direction. That is normal. The goal of visualizing is to get you on your intended path, which will continue to develop over time. Keeping focus by writing down what you intend to manifest will help keep you on a forward track. The realization phase happens over time, bit by bit, as your goals become clearer and more thoroughly internalized over time.

Once Joni and Olivia were talking again, Olivia agreed to meet Eddie. Over time, Olivia found that her discomfort with the age-gap evaporated. She appreciated how well Joni and Eddie and how good they were for each other. Olivia actually liked Eddie and was glad that her mother wasn't alone. By tapping into her well of positive emotions, Olivia was able to move away from her knee-jerk reactivity and engage in a conversation. This process led her to realize the closeness she desired with her mother.

Using the VIR Protocol, you will find many of your arguments de-escalate, and you will become both more wholehearted in how you feel and more detached from being caught up in what was once a compelling back-and-forth. The very act of reading this book and engaging in the exercises suggests that you're visualizing getting along better. You are now in this internalization process. Once you find your why, you can really start making changes in your response to conflict that will radically improve how you think and how you feel in your relationships. Your vision will be realized.

I'm Not Crying, You're Crying

Getting real with ourselves, or getting vulnerable, can feel really scary. It forces us to recognize our own weaknesses and face our fears head-on. It can be an unpleasant process, but it's the only way forward through entrenched conflict. This is especially true because of our natural tendency to externalize the root cause of what's gone awry. As discussed in the previous chapter, the source of our shame lies in our insecurities and our feelings of being less than.[i] When we acknowledge what's going on internally, at least to ourselves, we stand a chance of moving forward rather than spending years in the all-too-familiar endless argument loops.

In Part I, we learned that we need to own our part of the problem, including our own attitudes and habits that may be contributing to difficult dynamics. At this stage of the process, we may think we are clear on our role and our goals for the relationship. In Part II, we worked at developing better habits as we delved into understanding the emotional story, and in Part III we began to develop skills that to allow us to shelve or pause heated arguments and improve our situation by setting stronger boundaries. We may feel like we have done everything just as prescribed to improve a fraught dynamic—and yet, with some of our more challenging relationships, we still haven't seen any real change. Or maybe we have reverted to our old patterns without realizing it and need to do a little more work to get back on track.

Being truly vulnerable requires a lot of work because we're often accustomed to deflecting our part of the problem. As we discussed in the last chapter, rather than getting vulnerable, we often become reactive. This protective, defensive barrier is typically constructed over a lifetime for survival, but we lack the mechanism to let the barrier go when we no longer need it. Over time, it may begin to harm our relationships rather than protect us.

Our conflict cycles need to be examined in two ways: first, we need to consider what may be interfering with our ability to be vulnerable. It's often said that we're only as sick as our secrets. The worst person to keep secrets from is ourselves, and yet, we do it all the time. In my case, my proud inner narrative was keeping me protected from my own shame for not creating a fulfilling career.

During the early years of my marriage, I was trying so hard to be a good wife and mother that I forgot to take care of the rest of my life. In order to protect myself from feelings of inadequacy when I was unable to live up to my impossible standards, I blamed all my unhappiness on my husband. It is so much more comfortable to blame others for our failing dynamics that we rarely take the time to turn the mirror toward ourselves. This of course makes sense because seeing our own foibles is uncomfortable, but only by recognizing where we're stubborn, unrealistic, reactive, antagonistic, passive, or whatever we are, can we begin having different results.

Through getting acquainted with your most vulnerable

inner self, you can start to consider what may be interfering with your ability to shake off whatever you are rigidly holding onto.[ii] You may even consider whether loosening the emotional grip may serve and support your fraught relationship. Second (and more excitingly), once we see how our own nature, thoughts, action, and inaction are part of the problem, we must activate our own power to be a visionary. Getting real requires admitting our own weaknesses to ourselves. That's the most difficult part. But the payoff is immense, because once we note where we embody a weakness, we can visualize our relationships progressing forward.

Even today, Mitch doesn't see our early years the way I do. He says he was just working and doing what he had to do. He also didn't register any major changes in our relationship or his life since I started taking better care of myself. What he does see is that I am happier. Just as it only takes one person to damage a relationship, it too can only take one person to make it better.

Accessing Your Own Vulnerability

There are several steps to access your own vulnerability that are super easy, practically speaking. Emotionally, you may find this a bit more difficult than you may expect, but eventually it will become second nature.

- **Feel your feelings.** Noticing how you feel may bring up a sense of insecurity or discomfort. That is completely natural. This process of forcing ourselves to slow down may be challenging. However, the reward may be more honest inner discourse with yourself as well as stronger relationships with others. If you have the instinct to cry, allow yourself to experience the feelings, even the hard ones. Notice them and then, if they are not serving you, let them go. For instance, if you're the youngest child and you find you're often in dynamics where you're punching up, dismiss your knee-jerk tendency to over-write your self-worth affirmation with self-doubt and negative self-talk. Sometimes our feelings are a defensive reaction to a pattern established when we were children that no longer serves us. When you find it cropping up, notice it and create a self-worth affirmation to combat it, then release the shame you have been holding.

- **Use your "self-worth" affirmation.** Something simple such as "I am worthy" or "I deserve to be seen" can be very impactful. The point of this affirmation is to build a positive inner narrative that will promote your belief in yourself and in your inner value. You need to believe that you have value and can have better results (both for yourself and in your relationships). Invite the self-worth affirmation to permeate your thoughts.

- **Trust yourself to deal with disappointment.** When we are vulnerable, we open ourselves up to caring about outcomes, including failure. Invite yourself to trust that you can overcome adversity and failure. Reminding yourself of your value through the self-worth affirmations is so important, as it will help you through when you are feeling rejected or misunderstood. Remember that on the other side of each disappointment is success.

- **Remember that vulnerability communicates inner strength.** This does not mean you must overshare with people who are not in your trusted circle. Rather, it gives you the inner power to move away from blame and make more powerful, satisfying decisions. Instead of blaming your poor job performance on your boss, become vulnerable with yourself and consider what else is going on. Maybe you're a writer by profession but are continuously having your copy marked up and criticized by your supervisor. You could respond to this in a variety of ways. You could just decide your boss is a jerk and do nothing. You could quit your job and toss in the writer aspiration towel. Or you could decide to seek some constructive feedback from your boss. Maybe they have some great insights and, by accepting them, you will learn to improve your writing—or maybe you will learn that your writing style just isn't the right match for this position. Only by having the confidence to go in vulnerably and ask for constructive advice do you have a chance of transcending this relationship and having a more successful and rewarding experience at work.

Hillary and Simone Engaging with the VIR Protocol

Had Hillary or Sophie taken the time to use the VIR Protocol, they could potentially have saved their relationship and better supported each other's success. Had Hillary visualized her goals for her relationship with greater clarity, she could have gotten real and vulnerable with herself and instigated a conversation with Simone acknowledging her part of the interaction. If she had internalized this vision, even if Simone had not reciprocated, they could have parted ways on better terms. Rather than splintering the relationship, she could have visualized a cleaner parting and owned that she was agreeable by nature and that this tendency to be nonconfrontational may have been part of the problem. Had they had these conversations, maybe they could have agreed upon a compromise, such as Simone remaining for a few months for a smooth off-boarding process, and they could have left as friends. Perhaps, in return for Simone's extra months of assistance teaching Hillary the ropes of the business, Hillary would have shared more of the client list with Simone. Both businesses could have thrived, and more importantly they could have left open the possibility of remaining friends.

Secret Reveal: The Goal Is to Get Along Better, Not Perfectly

We cannot completely eradicate conflict from our lives. It will arise again and again, especially when left unchecked. That doesn't mean the skills we've learned through the YES Method did not work; it just means that it may be time for another check in with ourselves and with the world around us. With the VIR Protocol, in conjunction with the other strategies we've learned, we can reach a greater understanding of our emotional desires for ourselves and for our relationships with others. And we can stop these conflicts from spiraling into war, separation, or complete chaos.

As we talked about earlier in this book, one of the first steps in getting along is getting clear on what your relationship goals are. In my own life I found that to accomplish anything, the first thing I had to do was get crystal clear on the goal. Next, I had to internalize what it would look or feel like to accomplish the goal. Time and time again, with these two steps, whatever goal it was that I set out to accomplish, whether in my relationships (to get along better with my mother, husband, and children) or accomplishments (to write a book, grow my divorce firm, get more speaking gigs,) once I clearly articulated my goals and committed my whole self to internalize it, the results were realized.

Change Your Mind: Journaling for VIR

The VIR Protocol is not only useful in your relationship with others—it can also help to move the energy around in your own life. I experienced this shift when I added "author" and "speaker" into my job description in addition to "divorce lawyer" and "mediator." This process may sound "woo-woo," but it really works. What you are really doing is refocusing your energy so that your mind is naturally oriented toward the outcome you are seeking. While we may not be able to change our actual circumstances or the people we are sometimes stuck with due to these circumstances, with some pivots in thinking and attention, we can manifest better outcomes.

The next time you're feeling aggravated in a particular situation (or with a particular person) grab your journal and try this writing exercise.

1. **Visualize:** Write down how you wish to experience this interaction (or part of your life). Write down on the most granular level what it is you are looking to achieve. For

instance, let's say you want to feel more inspired by your work environment.

2. **Internalize:** Make a list of what inspiration feels like to you. Picture what you would be doing that would make you feel more inspired. Sticking with the example above, you may write down what you wish to accomplish; maybe you want to write a book, start a podcast, be the leader of a group, or earn more money. Close your eyes and imagine yourself doing the most outrageously exciting and inspiring version of what you are imagining (use your self-affirmations to push through that negative self-talk). And then get as detailed as possible.

   A very important note: It is essential that you do this on a daily basis. You are literally re-wiring your focus and attention. Your new, incrementally different way of seeing yourself in your life paves the way to you developing better, healthier relationships as well as more fulfilling circumstances.

3. **Realize:** As you internalize your visualizations into your being, it is likely that you won't actually have to *do* anything. The realization will present itself by virtue of you focusing a significant amount of attention in this positive direction. Realizing your vision is most likely when you truly embrace your vulnerability. Remember, we are only as sick as our secrets, and when we release them, if only to ourselves, we unleash our capacity to feel

better both within ourselves and in our relationships with others.

KEY TAKEAWAYS

- If you're still feeling stuck in a conflict after following the first three sections of this book, you'll find that getting vulnerable and tapping into the power of visualization is a great way to reframe a situation. Vulnerability yields both internal and external rewards, allowing us to be in touch with our feelings and creating opportunities for more honest and productive conversations with others.

- Practice feeling your feelings. Breathe intentionally three times a day. Create a self-worth affirmation, and integrate it into your breathing practice.

- By clearly visualizing our emotional wellness, we can begin to reframe our expectations for any particular relationship. VIR journaling exercises can help us to get vulnerable and to kick start the VIR Protocol. This process will remind us of the close foundational wisdom of needing to dig down further on the areas that may need the greatest amount of work.

- The VIR Protocol can do much more than simply help us to understand our values and needs; it will help us to become active visionaries for ourselves and for our futures.

CHAPTER NINE
Prevent Conflict from Spiraling into Chaos

Michelle recently called me for coaching and possibly legal representation. She told me she wasn't sure what to do in her marriage. On the one hand, she didn't want to burn down her family; her husband was kind and loving with her and their children, and he was a good provider. On the other hand, she felt stuck. On some days she was even profoundly unhappy. She felt that her world was falling apart but couldn't quite put a name to what was upsetting her. We set up a series of meetings over a short period to help her unravel what was going on for her. In conjunction with our meetings, she also met with a therapist who could help her work through her feelings through a mental and behavioral health perspective.

Our work together began with the YES Method, starting with how Michelle's habits or ways of thinking were interfering with her feelings of contentedness. She was not easily able to articulate what her role or contribution was in the conflict other than that she was critical. We then moved onto the E, for the emotional story. In that area she rated how she felt about the various areas in her life in including work, family, money, and her romance. We addressed each item one by one. Once she got clear on each area, she listened carefully to her inner voice around each thing that was upsetting her.

As we spoke, she began to cry. When we got to the family category, Michelle expressed that she was completely over-whelmed. In the last eighteen months, one of her children had been grappling with their gender identity. The other was strug-gling with alcohol and drug use. Both appeared to be suffering from low-level depression. She had tremendous guilt and con-fusion about how to understand her own feelings and how to best support her child to process her own identity. Plus, her worry about her other daughter's substance use was showing up for her no matter where she was and regardless of what she was doing. The concern over impending doom over both of their moods was hard for Michelle to shake. She also revealed that although she and her husband had never had an easy rela-tionship, things seemed to be turning for the worse as they disagreed on treatment plans for their daughters' depression. In addition, her mother had been diagnosed with stage-three ovarian cancer, and to top it all off, her kids' school was shut down due to coronavirus. It turned out that she, understand-ably, had a complete lack of clarity. There was just too much trauma for her to process all at once.

Her marital frustrations and disappointments seemed like the only part of Michelle's life over which she had agency. She came in to see me, inclined to ask her husband for a divorce. She asked me whether she should leave him. I advised her to consider whether her husband was the real issue or just the proverbial lowest-hanging fruit. The fact that the other issues were more long-term challenges was making Michelle less tolerant of her disagreements with him. It soon became clear that her marriage really wasn't the core cause of Michelle's upset. The desire to leave her husband may have been fueled at least in part because this was the one controllable unpleasant issue. However, I had a hunch that, even if she ultimately left him, their marriage might not be the issue to tackle first. Leaving him probably wouldn't improve their larger family issues—even after they divorced, their children would still be suffering, and Michelle's mother would still be sick.

At my suggestion, rather than immediately filing for divorce, Michelle shelved that conversation while she allowed the other parts of her life to evolve. Had she simply followed her impulse and left her husband, she may have inadvertently added fuel to the fire. Instead, we focused on prioritizing the issues and tackling them one at a time. On the one hand, when it came to her gender-questioning child, other than getting her help for the depression, there was nothing for Michelle to *do*. She had to just *be*. On the other hand, when it came to the depression and drug use of her other child, she wanted to intervene and offer whatever support was available. And yet, it all just felt too overwhelming. So, after several more sessions with me, she decided to first work on settling her own emotions around the chaos. Only then could she truly engage with the YES Method as it related to her husband.

Michelle methodically wrote down each issue that was upsetting her. She then made subcategories under each item naming her fears, distinguishing between what she could control and what she needed to accept. After a few weeks of making lists of each of the issues that were upsetting her, she started again at the beginning, clarifying that she felt completely overwhelmed because she was so accustomed to having to be everything to everyone.

Instead of looking at each issue as a separate manageable problem, she realized that she had been feeling like her life was a catastrophe. Every little thing that happened felt like the end of the world, because it was just one more thing on a huge, unmanageable pile. By looking at each upsetting issue as a separate, manageable problem, she was able to dispel her sense of impending doom and address the conflict in her life with equanimity. Her sleep gradually became less fitful and more restful. She was no longer exhausted from trying to get her daughter to stop using drugs. She decided to begin attending a support group for parents for teens with addiction, which gave her the support she needed just to get through not only with her daughter but also in her marriage. She learned to deal with each issue one at a time. Some of them entailed shifts in thinking. Others required that she behave differently. She separated out each of her problems and addressed each one at a time incorporating lists to deal with them in baby steps.

Michelle went from catastrophizing everything in her life to being able to listen to her own inner voice. But that alone was not enough. Michelle was pulled in way too many directions. She needed to figure out how to make time for herself as a regular part of her routine to reestablish her sense of inner peace. She committed to altering her habit of quickly reacting to all the triggers coming at her all at once, she opened herself to simply receive and respond to each problem as it arose. She engaged in the VIR Protocol and came to the conclusion that she needed to make time for self-care. This same message was supported in her parent support group. I taught her how to do the simple deep belly breathing from chapter 5 (page 125), and she created a self-care affirmation to combat feelings of overwhelm. In her case, she started with "I deserve self-care."

Last, by engaging in the alternative explanation exercise from chapter 3 (page 85), she took a step back from how she was feeling and listened to her inner voice. She began her process by having a conversation with her husband about her emotions surrounding their children's depression, and from there, the other conversations flowed. Last, she set boundaries by establishing a self-care schedule for herself that allowed her to take refuge from the abundant chaos in her life. She also created a manageable daily routine that blocked out periods of time for her to address each issue and then to set them aside, at least for the moment.

Maybe Michelle's story and struggle sounds familiar to you. Conflict tends to rain down on us all at once, making us feel powerless and overwhelmed by situations that, on their own, would feel manageable. In this penultimate chapter, I will show you how to stay grounded amid larger-scale conflict that can spiral into overwhelming chaos if left unchecked. In doing so, I will teach you how to find the perfect balance between marginalizing and catastrophizing conflict.

Minimizers and Catastrophizers

Most of us naturally tend to do one of two things when faced with overwhelming problems or conflict: we either marginalize the issue (sometimes even avoid it entirely) or we catastrophize it and become defensive, leading us to add to the conflict by lashing out at people around us and taking a zero-sum approach, becoming deeply attached to our positions (and thereby adding fuel to the fire).[i] Although they are both natural behavior patterns, in the end neither serve the cause of creating greater peace or calm. When we make everything into a drama or catastrophe, issues tend to grow in our mind, and we create problems where no issue would have arisen had we left well enough alone.[ii] Alternately, when we ignore each little issue or don't deal with something until it's too late, we allow things to build up so much that the overflow becomes unmanageable.

In my practice, I have often observed people on two ends of the reaction continuum—the minimizers and the catastrophizers. The minimizers are the ones who bury their heads in the sand and ignore all problems.[iii] They do well until there is an actual problem that needs to be handled. They tend to avoid and ignore problems for too long rather than dealing with the issue when it is still manageable. By failing to attend to smaller issues as they arise, they allow minor problems to grow, passively creating a chaotic snowball.

Minimizers are inclined to look at everything as "no big deal." They're the opposite of hypervigilant. They ignore issues and go about their business as though everything is hunky dory. Meanwhile, their bills are piling up, their partner ignores them, their kid is on drugs, or some other serious issues are piling up around them. The minimizers tend not to pay attention to anything until they *have* to. By the time the minimizer comes to me, their problems have often escalated to the point where it can be hard to see the path forward; they may be six months behind in their mortgage payments, or maybe their spouse is on their fourth affair, and they just can't turn a blind eye any longer.

On the other end of the spectrum are the catastrophizers. The catastrophizers view every little problem as a great drama. The catastrophizers are the more active creators of chaos. Catastrophizers may tend to be anxious by nature. They worry about all the what-ifs, and they may attempt to quell their anxieties by addressing anticipated worries as though they are actual problems. When left unchecked, they make choices that lead to the outcomes they were trying to avoid, fuel the fire of their anxiety, and ultimately make things worse.

Although Michelle was not a classic catastrophizer, her knee-jerk impulse to address her problems all at once impeded her ability to exercise good judgment and risked making matters worse. When she first came in to see me, she literally felt like the sky was falling. Her sense of utter helplessness was pervasive. In this flooded emotional state, she faced an increased risk of poor decision-making, which was likely to create further problems.[iv]

The snowball effect happens to catastrophizers and minimizers alike. The difference is that catastrophizers often create or exaggerate their problems or conflict, while the minimizers ignore it to the point where it becomes too out of control to ignore any longer. Regardless of where you or the people in your life may fall on this continuum, the solution is the same; unravel the spiral to decrease the sense of overwhelm. Even if you are a person who operates in one of these polarities, you can still dial back conflict with a solid understanding of how you can break complex issues down one by one into distinct issues that can then be addressed step by step, even in the face of high-stake conflict. Let's take a further look at how, when was are pressed, the spiral can happen to the best of us.

The Conflict Spiral

This phenomenon of conflict spiral comes into play in most of our lives. One small problem is either overblown or ignored for too long, and then things start to snowball out of control. During divorce, stress is at an all-time high and there are myriad conflict-ridden rabbit holes to go down. Emotions are often so out of whack that the ability to think clearly is compromised. Plus, the very divorce court process is practically designed to stir the emotional pot and create problems, by incentivizing litigants to point fingers at one another and cause more conflict rather than to navigate down a funnel of resolution. All too often, with flooded emotion, reactivity rather than reasonability drives the process.

Here's how the situation often unfolds: the client goes to the lawyer venting about how their life is unraveling right before their very eyes. The lawyer goes into fight mode and begins filing motions with the court accompanied by highly inflammatory affidavits (signed legal documents telling a one-sided version of the story). The other lawyer retaliates by responding and quite possibly escalating the argument with counter and cross claims. Next thing the client knows, they're embroiled in a messy court war when they could have been working on a more peaceful separation.

All too often, emotions, rather than rationality, drive the process—and all bets are off. Unfortunately, when left unchecked, our zealous advocacy has the capacity to cause unintended collateral damage. The adversarial process is practically designed to froth up conflict—and it's largely conflict-driven with little opportunity for de-escalation. Of course, sometimes court is necessary, but even when that is the case it is always the client's option to keep from one-upping their soon-to-be ex. Calling a ceasefire is always a viable alternative.

Though some relationships need to end, and there are situations where court is necessary, often the best way to resolve even the most heated conflict is to take a deep breath, a step back, and approach each issue one at a time. This is an important strategy to remember when dealing with conflict of any sort. Although conflict tends to rain down on us all at once, when you discipline yourself to keep grounded amid larger-scale conflict, you can prevent that snowball or spiral from causing overwhelming chaos.

Minimizers may enjoy a period of surface calm, but ultimately their avoidance of conflict allows small problems to spiral out of control, and they may be saddled with what feels like greater and more deeply-seated trouble. The additive cost of ignoring problems is that over time those problems may not disappear on their own. Minimizing the importance of any one small issue or conflict may be a great way to get through difficult situations in the short term, but beware of overdoing this. The unpaid bills add up.

Catastrophizers are not immune from creating chaos either. They're the exact opposite of the minimizers. They're the ones who wind up in court and experience each blow like a bludgeon. The trouble is that catastrophic thinking can lead the catastrophizer to create actual problems: a series of disagreements is blown out of all proportion until it becomes grounds for divorce. If you are already embroiled in a spiral of your own making, it is likely not too late to dial it back. Catastrophizers can feel very out of control even when things are reasonably balanced, but no matter how out of control your present spiral may feel, you can begin from right where you are, slowly and steadily until things begin to make sense and feel calm.

Strategies to Stop the Spiral

There are three great strategies that you can use to diffuse the conflict spiral: taking one issue at a time, in baby steps, and acknowledging the small stuff (which is more prevalent than we often realize).

1. One Issue at a Time

It is of utmost importance that you break out each individual issue—one at a time. Trying to address everything at once can create confusion and chaos. For example, Michelle's case conflated or confused her feelings of overwhelm about her children and her mother for a desire to get a divorce. By taking the time to distinguish these issues, she was able to reconnect with her husband and work together with him to address each of the other issues.

When troubles are overwhelming you, rather than allowing the confluence of unfortunate events to feel like a maelstrom, make a list of each item that is causing upset. Then address them individually, taking baby steps.

2. Baby Steps

Most of us are familiar with René Descartes's quote, "I think, therefore I am." But I find his lesser-known advice from step two of his *Discourse on Method* even more useful: "Divide each difficulty into as many parts as is feasible and necessary to resolve it."[v] What this means, essentially, is that most things we define as "difficult" are made up of a composite of many incremental challenges, conflicts, or problems; each of which can be overcome. When we begin to break down these issues, we can begin to see solutions one by one. The catastrophe is abated. This approach applies both to when we're experiencing a general internal problem and when we are caught up in interpersonal conflict.

3. Don't Sweat the Small Stuff

There's a reason Richard Carlson's *Don't Sweat the Small Stuff...and It's All Small Stuff* has sold more than five million copies.[vi] You can begin to exit conflictual situations and prevent useless arguments by recognizing when walking away (in whole or in part) makes sense. By carefully choosing your battles, recognizing what is really important, and making peace with imperfections (yours and others'), you can help to prevent creating the conflict spiral that can snowball into war all too easily.

Writing to Unravel the Spiral

If you are prone to getting caught in conflict spirals, it may be helpful to break down each of the specific scenarios that are upsetting you. In addition to cooling things off for catastrophizers, list-making and scheduling can help minimizers address problems before they spiral out of control, not just break them down after they have already done so: rather than bottling up those worries, write them down and schedule time whether daily or weekly to address them.

Make a list of these issues, such as:

- "I have too much responsibility."
- "My car keeps breaking down."
- "My ex-husband is always late with the child support check."
- "I have no time to exercise."

- "I never read anymore."
- "I feel alone all the time."

Once you have established the individual elements that are contributing to your spiral, you can begin to exercise your own agency by making small changes to your circumstances. In this example, once you have listed each of your issues, take a closer look at the things that are bothering you and dissect them into smaller steps by digging a bit deeper and breaking down what's going on in each category of trouble. Once again, grabbing your journal and dissecting what's really going on is going to do wonders for your well-being when things feel like they're spiraling out of control. As we've reviewed at other points in this book, making lists and journaling are great devices to use to get clarity.

Here is where separating "One Issue at a Time" from "Baby Steps" helps with organization. First, make a list where you separate your problems into distinct issues. For example, "I have too much responsibility" might be broken down further into each individual responsibility. Then you generate a list of steps to deal with each of the issues. For example, creating a schedule with blocks of time might help to deal with feelings of overwhelm, or maybe all that is necessary is to create the list, return to it when feelings of overwhelm threaten, and check off each item as it is resolved.

On the other hand, by organizing items in the list into

categories, several items could be addressed as a group. For example. "I have no time to exercise" and "I never read" might both be resolved by creating (and following) a schedule that includes a block of time for each.

Here is what unpacking "I have too much responsibility" may look like:

Make a list of all of the items you consider your responsibility. For example:

- Cooking
- Cleaning
- Kid schlepping
- Your home renovation
- Committee leadership
- Filing documents
- Caring for your mother
- Reporting to your supervisor
- Delegating to your staff
- Chairing meetings
- Teaching two yoga classes

Next to each item on the list, indicate which things are clearly delegable, which you actually need to do, and which you want to do. Draw a line through those items you can let go of. Then delegate what you can, and write the name of the person you are delegating to next to each of those items. In my case,

I need to show up and record my own podcast interviews, but creating social media graphics is something I can easily delegate. Of course, checking in with the people you delegate to may then be added to your list of responsibilities, but it should be one that requires considerably less time.

Get Comfortable Delegating

For the longest time, I handled every aspect of my business and my life on my own. In addition to being a divorce attorney, mediator, public speaker, and author, I felt like I also had to do my own marketing, research, outreach, website, search engine optimization—you name it, I did it. At home it was no different. For years I did the vast majority of the driving, organizing, shopping, and arranging for my family (notice I did not say cleaning, as I have always been comfortable letting someone else handle that)! It was insane. I always had my cell phone in my hand trying to keep up on everything at work while managing everything at home, half-assed at best.

I realized I blamed a lot of my stress on my husband. I felt that I *had to* do everything, when in fact, he is quite competent and could take care of a lot of the responsibilities that I was making my problem. Once I saw that he too could manage things and the world would not fall apart, I became more comfortable delegating at work.

You may have been doing so much yourself for so long that you don't even realize that you have the ability to hand off any particular task, but you would be surprised. Although it may take more time at the beginning to establish a new way of doing things, it will be worth it in the long run. While your kids may have grown accustomed to your carefully prepared caprese sandwich with mango slices on the side, they will probably make it through with school lunch or your partner's subpar food choices. (They may even prefer a lunch they've made for themselves.)

As you consider which responsibilities you wish to retain, and which you would prefer to offload, you will begin to see that others can pick up your slack, and not everything has to be done—at least not in the exact way that you would have done it. (Which to you may feel like *perfectly*.) Good enough may in fact be perfection! Just as we considered needs and wants all the way back in "Part II: The Emotional Story," once again ask yourself the ever-important question: *Why?* Is your desire to keep a particular responsibility a need or a want? Assess each of your obligations one at a time. Consider the best outcome if you keep the responsibility and the worst outcome if you keep the responsibility. Then consider the best and worst outcome if you delegate the task to someone else. Maybe it's something you can entirely let go; it really doesn't matter if the shirts are folded down the middle, even if you hate it that way. And, heaven forbid, it's also okay if every family member does their own laundry or grabs their own clean clothes from a messy pile on your bed. You just saved an hour a day (plus valuable real estate in your mind).

This method applies to anxiety management and to interpersonal problems that may be piling up, as it did in Michelle's case. To avoid allowing her problems to snowball and kicking her husband to the curb because of the apparent relief it would bring, Michelle considered each piece of what was causing her distress individually. This allowed her to step away from the catastrophizing outlook that was pervading her thoughts and back from the brink of divorce. When catastrophic thinking or reaction is happening, it's often said that a step back is the best way forward.

KEY TAKEAWAYS

- Consider how you look at your problems—the phrase "one thing at a time" is one that we all know, slowing down how you look at your problems will help make handling them more realistic.
- Unravel your spiral: make a list of each item that is causing upset, and then break each item down to its most manageable components incorporating the ever-important question *why* to help stave off the sense of overwhelm.

- Consider whether you are catastrophizing or minimizing issues in your life. Incorporate a breathing practice and mantra to calm the overwhelm and sort the issues.

CHAPTER TEN
Finding Equanimity

Getting along is an ongoing process. When all is said and done, at the end of the day, the reality is that there are rarely firm endings or "resolutions" to conflict: only management. But that's okay. What is important is that we open the opportunity to have strong, vulnerably honest discourse with the people and in the situations that matter most to us. Part of the problem is that we are overly attached to the idea of peace. Accepting that peace never lasts will help us manage conflict better, allowing us to put in the work to maintain our relationships through all the bumps in the road.

As we've seen throughout this book, the art of getting along involves two distinct parts: inner management and outer management. The inner part is how we think and feel about conflict. When we're in an emotionally excited state, we can't think clearly and we're often impulsively reactive rather than responsive. The outer part is how we act when we're uncomfortable or pushed to our limit. Our actions can in turn, create or avoid further conflict both with ourselves and with those around us. Only by looking at both the inner and outer parts in turn can we begin to change this dynamic in our lives, creating stronger relationships at home, at work, in the world, and within ourselves. Our long-term well-being is dependent on the quality of our relationships. We will always disagree with someone in our life, but we can do it in a better way. We need to always be asking ourselves whether our righteous indignation is worth the potential cost of the argument.

Nearly five years ago, my father fell very ill. We were extremely close; he was my greatest cheerleader but also a colossal pain in the ass (sorry, Dad). I was living in western Massachusetts with my three small boys and husband, and he was in Lenox Hill Hospital in New York City. Before I'd arrived at the hospital, he was in acute respiratory failure and was placed in a medically induced coma. For the next nine weeks, and with support from my brother, my husband, and my mother (my father's first ex-wife), I spent nearly all my time sitting with him at his bedside, navigating the doctors, his girlfriend, and his second ex-wife (my former stepmother). Fortunately, he regained consciousness and, although he was never again able to be fully independent, was able to live out the remainder of his life closer to my home in Massachusetts.

During the years he was sick, his care became my brother's and my responsibility. My brother and I have always been very close. He's hysterically funny (if not a *wee bit extra* in the sarcasm department) and always generous. But when it came to my father's care, we did not always agree. I am complicatedly both a minimizer and a catastrophizer (depending on the facts and circumstances), and this situation presented many crazy turns. At a certain point, our dynamic could have gone off the rails, but rather than digging into where we disagreed, we leaned into each of our respective strengths and found a way to split our responsibilities in a way that promoted our father's best care and fostered our close relationship. From my perspective, we are very lucky because we were inadvertently trained by the example set by our parents after their divorce to have strong conflict management skills.

Here's how the YES Method worked for us: We were both very aware of our respective strengths and weaknesses when it came to handling the hard issues that fell on our plates. We each recognized our own role and stayed in our own lanes. I was able to thoroughly research care options but didn't have the mental space to also create the budget to pay for care. My brother, on the other hand, was less available for drilling down into the details of what, exactly, my father needed in terms of care, but he was phenomenal at making all the financial logistics work. For the most part, my brother took care of managing and organizing the business side of things while I handled my father's day-to-day care. We supported each other as necessary to make everything run smoothly. We were both in touch with our own emotional story and were careful to satisfy both our own needs and our respective sense of love, duty, and obligation to our father.

My emotional need was to make sure I was an attentive daughter. To satisfy that, I did my best to ensure my father was engaged with people while far from his NYC home and that my family and I spent as much time as possible with him while he was still alive. My brother's emotional need was to be dutiful and loving in a more pragmatic way: by handling the finances. My brother was always supportive of me and managed things when I could not. We are each natural shelvers (maybe we were taught at a young age). When it comes to our communication with each other, we both have clear boundaries. We shelved conversations that were potentially going to become the firecrackers and waited to discuss the important parts when we were both feeling calm. When it came to getting along, to go deeper, I am definitely someone who wears their heart on their sleeve, and, even though my brother is comparatively reserved, he is also open in his own way. Because of our long-standing positive relationship, it was pretty easy to get to the root of what was going on for each of us when conflicts arose. Our father died a year ago as of this writing, and my relationship with my brother continues to evolve as we navigate new conflict that arises. We both want to spend quality time with our families together, but where we do it is sometimes an issue. Our kids love each other and sometimes they don't get along perfectly. Getting along is truly a constant give and take. Compromise, concessions, and allowances pave the way for us to both handle conflict between one another and to model it now for our children. Even when you are good at handling it, conflict truly is the gift that keeps on giving.

The Value of Equanimity

As we touched upon way back in the introduction, if you truly want to put your own mental and physical well-being at the center of your life, achieving a sense of equanimity in your relationships matters. How we get along with our partners, friends, family, coworkers, acquaintances, and even strangers matters. To get along with others, especially when we're pushed, we need to be balanced within ourselves. Balance is what allows us to take the beat and get clear on our role. It's what gives us the capacity to open a neutral space and listen. It gives us the strength to start establishing better boundaries

Equanimity is what gives the sense of inner balance. It is a feeling of calm and ease. Even when it's hard, developing this muscle is important, as it supports our ability to sustain healthy relationships over a lifetime. Without strong, long-term relationships with others, your own health suffers. So ironically, by doing the work to get along, even with difficult people and in hard situations, you are going to make your own life better.

The ongoing challenge is to look at each new conflict as an opportunity rather than a catastrophe. Even though at times we disagree, and we each can be stubborn and even a little headstrong, my brother and I agree that our relationship matters. A sense of equanimity, mental calmness, and composure prevails.

Using the YES Method, you now know that conflict is best handled when it's not seen as a zero-sum game. Instead, it's a win-win approach to even the most heated interpersonal differences. Sometimes a compromise can be easily reached. It begins with each person taking a step back to come forward. Rather than becoming heated, each partner can look at the options with equanimity. For example, while it may be important to one partner to always have the kitchen clean before going to bed for the night, the other partner might care more about sitting at the table together leisurely even if it gets too late to clean every last dish before turning in for the evening.

However the conflict is ultimately resolved, my hope for you is that you are able to face it with a sense of calm, taking the time you need to determine when to compromise, when to let go of the conflict, and when to shelve or even end the interaction. When dynamics feel challenging, accessing a sense of ease can feel inaccessible. Slowing down your mind is a great way to pave the path to relax. Here are some simple ways to invite equanimity into your life starting now.

The Importance of Sleep

It might sound obvious, but if you you're feeling off-kilter and out of balance, ask yourself if you've had enough sleep. For clear thinking, rest is essential. Sleep is restorative and allows for brain repair each day. If you have trouble sleeping, be sure you're taking care of your sleep hygiene.

- Stick to a consistent sleep schedule.
- Limit daytime naps.
- Eat healthy foods.
- Turn bright lights and devices off a half hour before you plan to sleep.
- Pay attention to what you eat—don't go to bed stuffed or hungry.
- Create a restful environment.
- Use a sleep meditation app.

Of course, sleep alone will not calm the anxious, reactive mind. However, what it will do is prime you for engaging with the YES Method in the best way possible. A well-rested mind is more accessible to self-reflect, change habits, listen to others, and build awareness of what is changeable and what must be accepted. Sleep aids should be used minimally. However, when necessary, under the care of a physician, they may be helpful in some cases.

Compromise, Concessions, and Allowances

Sometimes, letting go of a relationship is the only option. There are situations and dynamics that are not healthy, and in those cases, walking away is a must. But sometimes, in cases large and small, a compromise may still be the best way forward. If you find yourself inclined to cut someone off or to other-wise curtail a relationship, consider whether the relationship is important for you for other reasons.

Rachel, a rainmaker for a large investment firm, was court-ing John, a high-power banker, to get his business to her firm. After several weeks, she secured a coveted in-person meeting, which ended with him making a fantastic offer for her to bring back to her partners. As she was leaving, he said to her, "This never would have happened if you weren't so pushy." Rachel felt embarrassed at being called pushy. She felt ashamed and incredibly insulted. She did not want to walk away from the deal, yet she was uncomfortable with the inner compromise she found herself making. She wanted to tell him off, dress him down, and give him a robust education on what "pushy" looks like. Even though she was upset, she knew that was a bad idea. On the other hand, she didn't want to just walk out and say nothing. She decided to take the middle ground. Rather than demurring and thanking him for his time, she retorted, with a kind and firm smile, "Persistent."

Although John's comment bothered Rachel, she did not allow her impulse to punish him for using such a misogynis-tic word prevail. She gently stood up for herself and closed the deal. The concessions we choose to make are personal and are not one-size-fits-all. In this case, what John said is certainly a microaggression, and to some it could have been viewed as so antagonistic that it would not be worth the business. In Rachel's case, for a variety of reasons, including the fact that walking out on a deal that she'd spent so much time and energy making would have punished her far more than John, she decided to let it go. Sometimes, compromising (even with yourself) is the best way forward. Remember: you have the agency to decide when to compromise and when to walk away.

Compromise, of course, is where agreements are reached by both parties giving in—or making concessions to or allowances for what the other person wants. Concessions or allowances, on the other hand, are more of a one-way street. They're what we give to someone else with no obvious quid pro quo. We may make a concession simply because we feel like it's the right thing to do, or make allowances because we have no other choice. For instance, we may make, rightly or wrongly, more behavioral allowances for our neurodiverse child than we may for our other children. Most of the time, compromising will leave you feeling whole and satisfied. Concessions and allowances will leave you feeling like you did what had to be done. Sometimes, when two people make concessions and allowances to one another, in the aggregate they may add up to compromise. It can be a bit of a dance.

When my brother and I were navigating my father's care, we made many concessions to each other, which, in the aggregate, added up to compromise. I thought my father needed to be with familiar people every day. My brother wanted to make certain financial decisions. We may have had opinions about each other's separate choices but in favor of the balance, we gave permission to each other to do our best in our respective roles. That does not mean there were no conflicts. For instance, there was a time where I felt that my father needed more hired attendants for company (which related to his care, which was my lane) but it cost money (which was my brother's responsibility). Rather than have a *kaboom*, we talked it out and arrived at a mutually agreeable arrangement that both supported my father and our relationship with one another. There was an ongoing give and take. In a perfect world, both parties will do this, but sometimes, only one person in the dynamic has the wherewithal to see what's going on from the broader perspective.

Sometimes, especially in longer term relationships, concessions or allowances are necessary. For instance, it may be important to one partner to always arrive early, while the other partner is habitually late. The solution to this conflict may be to reach a compromise where you agree on certain categories when arriving early is essential (the airport) and when arriving late doesn't matter (a casual gathering). For engagements that don't fit easily into either category, the solution may be to agree to arrive within fifteen minutes of the start time, or you may prefer to simply arrive separately at each of your leisure. A concession is when you agree to something without gaining anything in return. For instance, if you are married to someone who is always running late, for the sake of getting along, you may just have to be okay showing up late for all but the most time-sensitive events. At first blush, it appears that when it comes to concessions, there is only give and no take, but on a deeper look concessions and allowances give us the gift of longevity and stability without significant cost.

Concessions and allowances are the tiny gives we all have to make on an ongoing, if not daily, basis in order to survive in a world where there are people who see things differently and want different things than we do. When we get most of what we want (to see the rom-com rather than the spy thriller that our partner would greatly prefer, for example) we have to give a little to maintain the balance. And so, to get to see our cinematic preference, we agree to go to our partner's favorite steakhouse when we really wanted sushi and sake. It's all about the giving and getting cycle. Tiny little break-ups that may otherwise erode a relationship can instead come through equally tiny little comings together.

Celeste was a professor at a well-known university. Her children were long grown and had their own lives, and at this point, her work was the center of her life. She gave it her all and it brought her tremendous joy. When her position at the university was going away, as they had decided to wind down her entire department, it was a major blow to her sense of fairness as well as to her sense of self. Rather than early retirement, the administration found a way for her to continue teaching a similar course of study under a different major. Losing many of her peers due to what felt like an extremely unfair process sent Celeste into questioning whether she was doing the right thing remaining at the college, and yet, for personal and financial reasons, leaving wasn't a real option. She allowed herself to feel disappointed for the working environment she lost. She made a list of what she needed to regain her sense of equanimity at work. She compromised her sense of fairness for what she knew she had to do for family and her own well-being, which was to keep her job. And she made allowances and concessions, if only intellectually, for her new colleagues' different ways of doing things. In this way, she was able to allow new healthy relationships to develop over time.

Hillary and Simone's Need for Equanimity

Hillary and Simone were backed into their corners and failed to recognize the relative importance of their relationship, cut off meaningful conversation without listening, failed to adjust their boundaries with each other, and did nothing to get vulnerable with themselves to change their path forward. They'd been friends for a long time, and they each really valued their friendship. Yet, they lacked the tools to work out their differences. Instead, they simply split. But let's assume Hillary and Simone had been able to salvage their friendship using the YES Method, with the goal of achieving equanimity through compromise, concessions, and allowances.

It could have gone so differently. Instead of canceling one another, either one could have sent an olive branch. This doesn't mean they would have become immediate besties as they once were, but with that shared history, they could have forged a path forward where they didn't entirely lose each other from their lives. It could have started with one of them simply sharing a funny meme with the other or sending a text. Or, if the fighting had been less, maybe, even though they disagreed on the path for their business, they could have continued to share a holiday meal together, just once a year, or meet at a familiar mutually beloved restaurant with their families just to open conversations. Even though having a business together wasn't meant to be for the long haul, their dynamic still had so many strengths. They trusted each other and shared a sense of humor. They also knew each other's families and were able to communicate with few words. Had they navigated this break up differently, as they went through life, they could have had the comfort of an old friend to lean on when times were rough and to celebrate with when things were going well.

Of course, even if Hillary and Simone had embraced the YES Method and navigated their conflict, new issues surely would have arisen over time. Maybe it would happen during a joint family vacation or a brunch with friends. Simone and Hillary had different temperaments and desires—and yet they could have remained friends and even supported each other's business endeavors. Rather than getting defensive and cutting off the relationship, they could have done something different. Understanding their own parts of the dynamic could have paved the way for better conflict management going forward. Over time, they could have checked in with themselves and each other to use the YES Method to help them conquer any obstacles that threatened to derail their friendship. They could have reacted to the conflict with equanimity by shelving when necessary and by being willing to compromise or by making concessions and allowances. Their relationship could have been given the chance to evolve. Instead, it withered away.

Create Space for a Calmer Today

The end of each conflict invites in a moment to rest and to enjoy a sense of calm. It allows us to notice when we feel okay, when we can lift the veil of armor. In every ending, there is a new beginning, a moment to feel energetically renewed. And yet, unless we truly cut off relationships (which is the answer only in rare circumstances), endings truly only unfold when we face conflict with equanimity, making ongoing compromises, concessions, and allowances.

For instance, in the divorce process, when the ink is dry on the Separation Agreement, that should be the endpoint for negotiation. Property distribution, debt allocation, support, custody, and all the relevant issues have been dealt with and there really isn't anything further to discuss. But life is full of nuance, and even when the basic rules of the post-divorce road have been settled, there's an ongoing need to continue fine-tuning or evolving the agreement. And of course, some people view this endpoint as an invitation to begin fighting anew. Unfortunately, divorce is the gift that, in some cases, keeps on giving. If you find yourself in an endless argument loop with an unreasonable person, it's particularly important that you get clear on your role, keep your own emotions in check, and shelve the conversations that can wait. You will garner better long-term outcome both in the moment and on an ongoing basis.

Conflict can leave us feeling empty, frustrated, disconnected, and alone. When conflict arises, reminding yourself that this is only one moment in time and that it will pass, you create opportunity for your emotions to settle. With this perspective, you can feel calmer, even in the present storm.

You can plan for a better more peaceful future by exploring how compromises, concessions, and allowances can give way to a stronger, more mature dynamic and enable your relationships to continue growing and evolving.

Compromise or Concession Thought Exercise

Here is a quick list of ideas to consider if you're just not sure where if you're not sure where your relationship is in balance on the continuum from doormat to steamroller.

For the purpose of this exercise, "partner" here refers to the other person in the relationship you're evaluating, whether they're your spouse, relative, friend, coworker, etc.

STEAMROLLER	BALANCED	DOORMAT
You expect and demand your partner to work within your schedule.	You are open to negotiating schedule conflicts.	Your always bend to work within your partner's schedule.
Regardless of circumstance, getting your way is the only acceptable outcome.	You are comfortable asking for what you need and listening to what your partner needs.	You feel guilty when you ask to do something for you or give something to you
You do what you please and know your partner is always there to clean up your mess (physically, emotionally, financially).	You take care of your own responsibilities and clean up after yourself (physically, emotionally, financially).	You're always cleaning up their mess and taking care of their responsibilities and making excuses for their failures or shortcomings.
When your partner disappoints you, you aggressively and directly let them know it.	You are able to respectfully let your partner know when they have disappointed you.	You are uncomfortable calling out your partner's faults and tend to avoid confrontation.

STEAMROLLER	BALANCED	DOORMAT
Being honest and frank is more important than trying to protect your partner's feelings.	You are comfortable discussing uncomfortable topics and are willing to hear each other out.	Harmony with your partner matters more than expressing your thoughts.
You do whatever you need to do to get your way.	You make concessions or compromises but still hold your ground on important issues when you don't see eye to eye.	You habitually swallow your pride to get along.
Being right is the most important thing to you.	There's always a solution that more or less satisfies everyone.	Peace matters more than anything else.
The only satisfactory way to end a discussion is by having your partner agree with your opinion.	You can agree to disagree, compromise, or make concessions and still feel satisfied with the outcome	You consistently defer to their thoughts and opinions regardless of your own thoughts and feelings.

While the nature of this inquiry is quite simple, it's a great way to get you to begin noticing your habitual responses to conflict. As you navigate each interaction, ask yourself to consider what different responses you may have to elicit a more balanced outcome.

Healthy relationships have a balanced compromise system of give and take over time. Sometimes concessions and allowances, which are one-sided by definition, are necessary to create this balance in the long term. However, if you find yourself constantly giving in because you believe it's easier to just "go with the flow," beware: you could lose yourself. If that describes you, over time you may resent your role in any given relationship. Your habit of continuously telling yourself that your point of view or desire doesn't really matter can have diminishing returns. Concessions by only one party in the relationship that happen repeatedly for "the good of the relationship" can actually erode your dynamic over time by creating an unbalanced dynamic.

On the other hand, if you are always getting your way, although that may feel good personally, consider the negative impact that this imbalance brings to your relationship. Create space for others to air their thoughts, opinions, and desires. By making that space, you create opportunity for consensus and for your relationship to grow. Whether you are giving or taking too much, it's time to start the YES Method right back at step one and ask yourself how you're contributing to or creating these issues.

Some relationships need to end. But much of the time, by engaging with the YES Method, we can get along. If not perfectly, at least better. Getting along is truly an art. We need to address how we think, feel, and act. In taking the time to go through all of these processes, we create opportunity for feeling more whole in our lives, in our relationships and, in the world.

KEY TAKEAWAYS

- Your own health is supported by achieving inner calm or balance or a sense of equanimity in your relationships.
- Compromise is a necessary daily process, and this book offers you thoughts exercises that will help you commit to compromise—even when it's difficult.
- Sometimes concessions and allowances are necessary to maintain a relationship over the long term, but beware of allowing relationship dynamic to become unbalanced.
- Return to the YES Method as often as you need it, until the steps become as obvious as breathing and a part of your daily growth.

Afterword

When cooperation is not possible, rather than dismantling the relationship, remember that often you can operate in a parallel structure. Recall the tools from the YES Method that you have at your disposal when reaching consensus proves impossible.

Managing expectations, recognizing limitations, and considering emotions that do not always work in concert will hold you in good stead. Getting along and feeling good in all your life circumstances will sometimes rely on a well-choreographed dance, taking that step back to recognize when it makes sense to push, pull, and prod and when to walk away. When conflict feels impossible, reflect on your role, consider the emotional story, and shelve the conversation or relationship when leaning will result in a senseless argument loop.

Remember, *The Secret to Getting Along* is that while in most instances you'll never get along perfectly, most of the time, using the YES Method, you can get along *better*.

Reading Group Guide

These discussion questions correspond to the four different parts of *The Secret to Getting Along (And Why It's Easier Than You Think!)*.

Part I: Your Role in the Conflict

1. Are there important relationships in your life that you are unhappy with or ones that you think can be improved?
2. What destructive behavior patterns do you have that are interfering with your relationships? Do you steamroll? Bury your head in the sand? Stir the pot? Catastrophize? Minimize?
3. What are the obstacles that prevent you from applying the changes that need to be made in order to improve your relationship?
4. From the other person's perspective, might there be things that you do or say that they might perceive negatively?

Part II: The Emotional Story

1. What actions or words by other people trigger you? When your emotions are running high, take notice: how do you act? How do you react?

2. How do you tackle problems that arise in your life? Do you tend to catastrophize or minimize?

3. When you are in conflict with another person, do you argue with them to get what you want or do you engage in meaningful conversation to ensure an acceptable outcome for both parties?

4. Do you notice when you are being positional in your relationships?

5. How can you get to the core of what you need so that you can peacefully resolve your conflicts?

6. How does your inner narrative shape the way you see and think about your relationships and the world around you?

Part III: Shelving Heated Conversations

1. Which of your boundaries can you soften? Do you have boundaries that need to be firmer? When do you have a hard time saying no? What can you do to take a break without causing the relationship to break down?

2. Are there ongoing heated conversations or difficult discussions in your life or relationship that can benefit from shelving?

3. What activities, whether passive or active, do you find most enjoyable or relaxing? How often do you engage in these activities?

4. What actions or words by other people tend to put you on the defensive?

Part IV: Yes, You Can Get Along

1. Visualize the ideal situation for your most important or most conflict-filled relationship. What does it look like? What does it *feel* like?

2. How in tune are you with your feelings? Are you able to verbalize them and describe them—even just to yourself?

3. What is the positive affirmation or mantra that you need in order to re-center and encourage yourself in difficult situations?

4. How committed are you to finding the just-right balance in your relationships, and how important is it *for your wellbeing* to keep the relationships that you are seeking to restore balance to?

Further Reading

The Gifts of Imperfection: Let Go of Who You Think You're Supposed to Be and Embrace Who You Are by Brené Brown

The Power of Habit: Why We Do What We Do in Life and Business by Charles Duhigg

Mindset: The New Psychology of Success by Carol Dweck

Crucial Conversations: Tools for Talking When Stakes Are High by Joseph Grenny, Ron McMillan, Kerry Patterson, and Al Switzler

Set Boundaries, Find Peace: A Guide to Reclaiming Yourself by Nedra Tawwab

You're Not Listening: What You're Missing and Why It Matters by Kate Murphy

Breath: The New Science of a Lost Art by James Nestor

High Conflict: Why We Get Trapped and How We Get Out by Amanda Ripley

Better Than Before by Gretchen Rubin

Practicing Mindfulness: 75 Essential Meditations by Matthew Sockolov

Getting to Yes by Roger Fisher and William Ury

Never Split the Difference by Chris Voss and Tahl Raz

Acknowledgments

Thank you to my clients and mentors, without whom there would be no book.

Thank you to my agents and their team at Aevitas Creative Management; Jen Marshall for her brilliant straight talk, vision, and friendship, Justin Broukaert for his metered optimism, wit, and for helping me to bring yet another book to market, and Erin Files for securing foreign rights in China and beyond.

I am so grateful to Alexis Gargagliano, my developmental editor who got my creative juices in full gear way back when this project was in ideation, and to my dear friend and proposal editor, Wendy Foster, for her incredibly detailed work bringing this project home into a cohesive product. Without these two, I may still be with my thoughts and words swirling not all the way cohesively on the page.

Thank you to my incredibly hands on, sharp, and kind book editor Anna Michels for your time, care, and attention (and for making time to show up at my TEDx!) and the entire Sourcebooks team for bringing this book to market.

I am so grateful for so many others who helped support me in countless ways. Georgia Uy, who does so much for me behind the scenes. Jill Sherer Murray, a creative genius and my personal cheerleader. Susan Guthrie my colleague, dear pal, and mentor (and yes, you *can* make true friends on social media!). Lauren Hollander, LISCW, for making time to review each page of content with painstaking patience.

Biggest thanks to Dana Weiner and Atara Twersky, my teachers, soul mates, fashion consultants and lifelong besties who got me through COVID (and so much more). To Pearl Lockwood, Lynne Strasfeld, Cheryl Knopp, Jennifer Bracco, and Danielle Demaio for your gift of listening—especially in the hardest of times.

And, to all the rest of my incredibly vibrant, wise, supportive, powerful female friends; Lisa Goldstein, Lisa Kaufman, Lisa Potash, Andrea Cohane, Pauline Cacucciolo, Katrien van Eetvelde, Amy Shatz, Caryn Brause, Leslie Skantz, Valerie Vignaux, Robin Rudowitz, Jill Falcone, Mara Hatzimemos, Renee Wetstein, Amy Richter, Jessica Berrien, Jenny Yang, Tina Finneran, Julie Jurman, Kim Lehrman, Beth Notar, Karen Soren, Elissa Miller, and Trish Peterson (who I've known since we were 8)! I truly cannot imagine this journey without each of your thoughts, perspective, laughter, honesty, and energy spent listening to me ramble and enduring my sometimes disjointed ideas and meandering musings over many decades. You enrich my life in myriad ways, and I am eternally grateful to each of you.

Thank you to my parents, Peter and Ruth, my stepfather, Terry, my grandparents, Ilse, Walter, Sally, and Joe, and to my aunts and uncles for endless love and support and for being wonderful teachers and role models. I am also grateful for my dear cousins, Peter, Larry, Steven, Camilla, Adam, Barbara, and David, who have stuck by my side for decades, even when we disagree (which is more often than you may imagine). Thank you to my siblings, Marcello, Caryn, and Carol, the best confidantes, sidekicks, and friends at every turn. Thank you for being with me from the start. Life with each of you is the best trip I could ever have asked for.

And of course, my deepest gratitude goes to my husband, Mitch, and to our three funny, loving, and inspiring sons, Reid, Max, and Zac who never disappoint, engage at every turn, and who always keep me focused on the importance of getting along.

I love you all.

Notes

Introduction

i   "COVID-19 pandemic may have increased mental health issues within families," *EurekAlert! Online*, April 12, 2021, https://www.eurekalert.org/news-releases/527486.

ii Britannica, T. Editors of Encyclopedia, "conflict," *Encyclopedia Britannica*, February 3, 2014, https://www.britannica.com/scienceconflict-psychology.

iii Susan Krauss Whitbourne, Ph.D., "5 Reasons We Play the Blame Game," *Psychology Today*, September 19, 2015, https://www.psychologytoday.com/us/blog/fulfillment-any-age/201509/5-reasons-we-play-the-blame-game.

iv Benjamin Garnder and Amanda L. Rebar, "Habit Formation and Behavior Change," *Oxford Research Encyclopedia of Psychology*, April 26 2019, https://oxfordre.com/psychology/view/10.1093/acrefore/9780190236557.001.0001/acrefore-9780190236557-e-129.

Chapter One: Recognize Your Role

i   Kimberly Holland, "Amygdala Hijack: When Emotion Takes Over," Healthline, September 17, 2021, https://www.healthline.com/health/stress/amygdala-hijack#symptoms.

ii   Cecile Andrews, interview by Julie Croteau, "Social ties are good for your health," *BeWell*, accessed August 16, 2021, https://bewell.stanford.edu /social-ties-are-good-for-your-health/.

iii   Elle Hunt, "What does it mean to be a 'Karen'? Karens explain," *The Guardian*, May 13, 2020, https://www.theguardian.com/lifeandstyle/ 2020/may/13/karen-meme-what-does-it-mean.

iv   Kate Murphy, *You're Not Listening: What You're Missing and Why It Matters* (New York: Celadon Books, 2020).

v   Gwen Moran, "How To Be Objective When You're Emotionally Invested," Fast Company, December 9, 2014, https://www.fastcompany .com/3039453/how-to-be-objective-when-youre-emotionally-invested.

vi   Nadine Jung et al., "How Emotions Affect Logical Reasoning: Evidence from Experiments with Mood-Manipulated Participants, Spider Phobics, and People with Exam Anxiety," *Frontiers in Psychology* 5 (October 2014), https://doi.org/10.3389/fpsyg.2014.00570.

Chapter Two: Harness Your Habits

i   Society for Personality and Social Psychology, "How we form habits, change existing ones," *ScienceDaily*, accessed August 17, 2021, https:// www.sciencedaily.com/releases/2014/08/140808111931.htm.

ii   Benjamin Garnder and Amanda L. Rebar, "Habit Formation and Behavior Change," *Oxford Research Encyclopedia of Psychology*, April 26 2019, https://oxfordre.com/psychology/view/10.1093/acrefore/9780190236557. 001.0001/acrefore-9780190236557-e-129.

iii   Elaine N. Aron Ph.D., "The Power of Inner Silence for the Highly Sensitive," *Psychology Today*, June 18, 2018, https://www.psychologytoday .com/us/blog/the-highly-sensitive-person/201806/the-power-inner -silence-the-highly-sensitive.

iv   Marla Tabaka, "Most People Fail to Achieve Their New Year's

Resolution. For Success, Choose a Word of the Year Instead," *Inc.*, January 7, 2019, https://www.inc.com/marla-tabaka/why-set-yourself-up-for-failure-ditch-new-years-resolution-do-this-instead.html.

v   Madhuleena Roy Chowdhury, BA, "The Science & Psychology Of Goal-Setting 101," *Positive Psychology*, February 15, 2022, https://positivepsychology.com/goal-setting-psychology/.

Chapter Three: Neutrality Is the Portal to Possibility

i   Sylvia Xiaohua Chen, "Harmony" in *The encyclopedia of positive psychology* (London: Blackwell Publishing, 2009), https://www.researchgate.net/publication/256649929_Harmony.

ii   Jerry Kolber and Bill Margol, creators, *Brain Games*, hosted by Keegan-Michael Key (2011; Los Angeles: Magical Elves Productions/National Geographic), https://www.disneyplus.com/en-gb/series/brain-games/7KcTpCZQnLa0.

iii   Jeremy Shapiro Ph.D., "Finding Goldilocks: A Solution for Black-and-White Thinking," *Psychology Today*, May 1, 2020, https://www.psychologytoday.com/us/blog/thinking-in-black-white-and-gray/202005/finding-goldilocks-solution-black-and-white-thinking.

iv   Rongjun Yu, "Stress potentiates decision biases: A stress induced deliberation-to-intuition (SIDI) model," *Neurobiol Stress*, vol. 3 (2016): pp. 83–95, accessed August 16, 2021, https://www.ncbi.nlm.nih.gov/pmc/articles/PMC5146206/.

v   Laura B. Luchies et al., "Trust and Biased Memory of Transgressions in Romantic Relationships," *Journal of Personality and Social Psychology* 104, no. 4 (2013): pp. 673–694, https://doi.org/10.1037/a0031054.

Chapter Four: The "What" versus the "Why"

i   "The Quiet Power of Empathic Listening," Mental Health First Aid,

September 27, 2017, https://www.mentalhealthfirstaid.org/2017/07
/quiet-power-listening/.

ii   Julianne Ishler, "How to Release 'Emotional Baggage' and the Tension
      That Goes with It," Healthline, September 16, 2021, https://www
      .healthline.com/health/mind-body/how-to-release-emotional
      -baggage-and-the-tension-that-goes-with-it#What-does-it-mean-to
      -have-trapped-emotions?.

iii   P Wesley Schultz and Alan Searleman, "Rigidity of Thought and
      Behavior: 100 Years of Research," *Genetic, Social, and General Psychology
      Monographs* 128, no. 2 (May 2022): pp. 165–207, https://pubmed.ncbi
      .nlm.nih.gov/12194421/.

iv   Daniella Laureiro-Martínez and Stefano Brusoni, "Cognitive
      Flexibility and Adaptive Decision-Making: Evidence from a
      Laboratory Study of Expert Decision Makers," *Strategic Management
      Journal* 39, no. 4 (2018): pp. 1031–1058, https://doi.org/10.1002
      /smj.2774.

v   Carol S. Dweck, *Mindset: The New Psychology of Success: How We Can
      Learn to Fulfill Our Potential* (New York: Ballantine Books, 2008).

Chapter Five: You Can Control Your Inner Narrative

i   Jordyn Posluns, "What Is the Internal Narrative Phenomenon?"
      WorldAtlas, February 28, 2020, https://www.worldatlas.com/articles
      /what-is-the-internal-narrative-phenomenon.html.

ii   Ben Alderson-Day and Charles Fernyhough, "Inner Speech:
      Development, Cognitive Functions, Phenomenology, and
      Neurobiology," *Psychological Bulletin* 141, no. 5 (May 25, 2015): pp.
      931–965, https://doi.org/10.1037/bul0000021.

iii   Daniel Kahneman, "Of 2 Minds: How Fast and Slow Thinking Shape
      Perception and Choice [Excerpt]," *Scientific American*, June 15, 2012,

https://www.scientificamerican.com/article/kahneman-excerpt
-thinking-fast-and-slow/.

iv   Malcolm Gladwell, *Outliers: The Story of Success* (New York: Back Bay
      Books, 2019).

v   Malcolm Gladwell, *David and Goliath: Underdogs, Misfits, and the Art of
      Battling Giants* (New York: Turtleback Books, 2015).

vi   "Malcolm Gladwell on the Advantages of Disadvantages," Knowledge@
      Wharton, December 3, 2013, https://knowledge.wharton.upenn.edu
      /article/david-goliath-malcolm-gladwell-advantages-disadvantages/.

vii   Tracey Anne Duncan, "How to Stop Your Inner Monologue from Running
      Your Life," Mic, February 5, 2020, https://www.mic.com/life/what-does
      -your-internal-monologue-say-about-your-mental-health-21777794.

viii Victoria Lemle Beckner Ph.D., "The Key Skill We Rarely Learn: How to
      Feel Your Feelings," *Psychology Today*, October 12, 2020, https://www
      .psychologytoday.com/us/blog/harnessing-principles-change
      /202010/the-key-skill-we-rarely-learn-how-feel-your-feelings.

ix   Jon Jaehnig, "What Is Inherited Behavior?," BetterHelp, June 16, 2021, https://
      www.betterhelp.com/advice/behavior/what-is-inherited-behavior/.

x   Prabhakararao   Sampthirao,   "Self-Concept   and   Interpersonal
      Communication," *International Journal of Indian Psychology* 3, no. 3
      (April 2016), https://doi.org/10.25215/0303.115.

xi   Monisha Pasupathi et al., "The Feeling of the Story: Narrating to Regulate
      Anger and Sadness," *Cognition and Emotion* 31, no. 3 (January 8, 2016):
      pp. 444–461, https://doi.org/10.1080/02699931.2015.1127214.

Chapter Six: Shelving and Boundaries Will Set You Free

i   Megan LeBoutillier, *"No" Is a Complete Sentence* (New York: Ballantine
      Books, 1995).

ii   Ilana Herzig, "Saying No Isn't Easy," *Psychology Today*, September 4, 2018, https://www.psychologytoday.com/us/articles/201809/saying-no-isnt-easy.

iii   Shoba Sreenivasan and Linda E Weinberger, "What Happens When People Who Always Say 'Yes' Say 'No?'" *Psychology Today* (Sussex Publishers, September 16, 2016), https://www.psychologytoday .com/us/blog/emotional-nourishment/201609/what-happens-when -people-who-always-say-yes-say-no.

iv   Jennifer King Lindley, "This Is Why It's So Hard to Say No," *Real Simple*, December 27, 2016, https://www.realsimple.com/magazine-more /inside-magazine/life-lessons/learn-to-say-no.

v   William Ury, *The Power of a Positive No: How to Say No and Still Get to Yes ; Save the Deal, Save the Relationship—and Still Say No* (New York: Bantam Books, 2008).

Chapter Seven: Defensiveness Is the Enemy of Resolution

i   Robert R. Stains, "Reflection for Connection: Deepening Dialogue through Reflective Processes," *Conflict Resolution Quarterly* 30, no. 1 (2012): pp. 33–51, https://doi.org/10.1002/crq.21053.

ii   T. Editors of Encyclopedia Britannica, "Defense Mechanism," *Encyclopedia Britannica*, January 31, 2020, https://www.britannica .com/topic/defense-mechanism.

iii   Becca Sangwin, "Why We Need to Stop Playing the Blame Game," The Gottman Institute, March 13, 2017, https://www.gottman.com/blog/why -we-need-to-stop-playing-the-blame-game/.

iv   Manfred F. R. Kets de Vries, "Don't Let Shame Become a Self-Destructive Spiral," *Harvard Business Review*, June 1, 2017, https://hbr.org/2017/06 /dont-let-shame-become-a-self-destructive-spiral.

v   Neel Burton, "The Psychology of Embarrassment, Shame, and Guilt,"

Psychology Today, August 26, 2014, https://www.psychologytoday .com/us/blog/hide-and-seek/201408/the-psychology-embarrassment -shame-and-guilt.

vi   Sara Lindberg, "Projection in Psychology: Definition, Defense Mechanism, Examples," Healthline, September 15, 2018, https://www .healthline.com/health/projection-psychology#defense-mechanism.

vii Andrea Brandt, "How Reactive Behavior Damages Your Relationships," *Psychology Today*, October 1, 2018, https://www .psychologytoday.com/us/blog/mindful-anger/201810/how-reactive -behavior-damages-your-relationships.

viii Kim Pratt, "Psychology Tools: How to Take a 'Time out,'" HealthyPsych, May 23, 2017, https://healthypsych.com/psychology-tools-how-to-take -a-time-out/.

ix   Diane Musho Hamilton, "Calming Your Brain During Conflict," *Harvard Business Review*, December 22, 2015, https://hbr.org/2015/12 /calming-your-brain-during-conflict.

Chapter Eight: The VIR Protocol: Your Secret Weapon

i   Shahram Heshmat, "5 Factors That Make You Feel Shame," *Psychology Today*, October 4, 2015, https://www.psychologytoday.com/us/blog /science-choice/201510/5-factors-make-you-feel-shame.

ii   Dianne Grande, "Emotional Vulnerability as the Path to Connection," *Psychology Today*, February 24, 2019, https://www .psychologytoday.com/us/blog/in-it-together/201902/emotional -vulnerability-the-path-connection.

Chapter Nine: Prevent Conflict from Spiraling into Chaos

i   Rebecca Joy Stanborough, "Cognitive Distortions: 10 Examples of

Distorted Thinking," Healthline, December 18, 2019, https://www
.healthline.com/health/cognitive-distortions#thought-origins.

ii   "Apa Dictionary of Psychology," American Psychological Association,
accessed March 28, 2022, https://dictionary.apa.org/catastrophize.

iii "Apa Dictionary of Psychology," American Psychological Association,
accessed March 28, 2022, https://dictionary.apa.org/minimization.

iv   Jennifer S. Lerner et al., "Emotion and Decision Making," *Annual
Review of Psychology* 66, no. 1 (January 3, 2015): pp. 799–823, https://
doi.org/10.1146/annurev-psych-010213-115043.

v   René Descartes and John Veitch, *A Discourse on Method* (London: J. M.
Dent, 1969).

vi   Richard Carlson, *Don't Sweat the Small Stuff and It's All Small Stuff: Simple
Ways to Keep the Little Things from Taking Over Your Life* (Thorndike,
ME: G. K. Hall, 1998).

Index

About the Author

Gabrielle Hartley, Esq., is a top divorce lawyer and mediator known for resolving 99% of her cases at the negotiation table. She is a sought-after speaker on conflict resolution, author of *Better Apart: The Radically Positive Way to Separate,* and creator of *The Better Apart Blog.*

Gabrielle is a recognized expert in the positive divorce and conflict resolution space across media outlets such as the *New York Times, Real Simple, Forbes, Vice,* the *New York Post,* and *U.S. News and World Report.* She can be heard on dozens of podcasts, radio shows and is a regular guest on NBC's *Mass Appeal.* She's a co-chair of the American Bar Association Section of Dispute Resolution's Mediation Committee. Her popular TEDx talk, "The Secret to Getting Along Is Easier than You Think," can be viewed on YouTube. She lives in Northampton, Massachusetts with her husband and three sons.

Mediate or consult with Gabrielle at gabriellehartley.com.